ORDINARY SEAMAN

ORDINARY
SEAMAN

JOHN GORDON

WALKER BOOKS
LONDON

For Sylvia, the girl at the heart of it.

First published 1992 by Walker Books Ltd
87 Vauxhall Walk, London SE11 5HJ

Text © 1992 John Gordon
Cover illustration © 1992 Carolyn Piggford

First printed 1992
Printed and bound in Great Britain by
Billings & Sons Ltd, Worcester

British Cataloguing in Publication Data
A catalogue record for this book is
available from the British Library.

ISBN 0-7445-2106-8

If I walked straight slap
Headlong down the road
Towards the two-wood gap
Should I hit that cloud?
Ivor Gurney

CONTENTS

WATER

The night was so black that although I could hear the tide slur along the ship's side I could not see the water a few feet below. We were well offshore, tied up to a buoy in midstream, and only the occasional glint of a hooded headlight showed where Harwich lay in the blackness. There had been no air raids anywhere along the coast, no flash of bomb or gun, not even an angling searchlight to distract the man on watch.

I was bored. My mate Molyneux had gone below where they were brewing a new can of tea on the messdeck, and I was on watch alone. I went to the ship's side and leant on the rail ... but someone had removed a section, and I leant into empty air.

I was nineteen but still only in the middle of my teens because I had joined up straight from school and, whatever else the Navy had taught me, it had not made me grow up. It fed me, clothed me and made all my decisions for me. But as I made a spread-eagled somersault into the blackness, that night in Harwich, I was on my own.

I hit the water upside down but came to the surface with my cap still on my head. It was January and a frosty night so I was wearing a heavy watch-coat down to my ankles and two pullovers over my other clothes. Now they were waterlogged and the tide was moving me. There was no time to strip off but I just managed to paddle to a rope fender that hung down to the waterline.

I tried to climb but could get no more than half out of the water, so I wrapped my submerged legs around the fender and clung on, wondering what to do next.

Characters in cartoons have "Help!" bubbles coming out of their mouths so I shouted "Help!" although that soon sounded so foolish that I changed it to a more seamanlike "Ahoy there!" It made no difference; no one came, and I dangled a hand in the water to pass the time and see how cold it was. I couldn't feel a thing.

Molyneux took his time and I had more or less ceased to shiver when at last I heard his footsteps on the upper deck.

"Ahoy!" I shouted, and he shone the watchman's torch down on me.

"What the hell are you doing down there, Gordon?" he said, and couldn't move for laughing.

Eventually he got a Jacob's ladder down to me but I couldn't even grip the wooden rungs. I was still struggling when a liberty boat came alongside and some of my shipmates, coming back from shore leave, lifted me on board.

On a minesweeper there are no bathtubs for ratings, but the wardroom had one and I was allowed to soak in hot water until the numbness left my limbs, then I went to bed for a couple of hours and was back on watch at four a.m.

Water has put its mark on several stages in my life. One of them was long before the Navy, when my family moved from the North to the flat Fens of East Anglia. It was two years before the war, and I was twelve.

My father, who was a teacher and part-time tobacconist in his own father's shop, brought us south when his school had to cut back its staff and he had lost his job. He went ahead of us to his new school in Wisbech, and my mother brought the rest of us to join him some months later.

I remember my mother's anxiety. She had wept when she was scrubbing the bare floorboards of our empty house in Jarrow to leave it clean for the new people, and all through the journey she fretted over her four children. I was the eldest, with two young brothers and a little sister, a small herd of Geordies who knew nothing about where we were going.

My grandfather had told me, "They grow so much fruit down there, man, that you'll be able to pluck bananas from the hedges." What he had never said was that the Fens were flat.

Every scrap of variety drained out of the landscape as we came to the Fens just as the sun was going down. The land was so flat we could have been on an inland lake, and the view out of every window was so utterly changeless that our train seemed to stop moving long before it drew into Wisbech. It was the platform itself that seemed to come out of the dark and haul itself alongside us like an old barge, clanking and hissing.

My father took us to our new home by taxi. Wisbech is cut in two by a river, and as we crossed the bridge we had our first real glimpse of the town. A full tide from the Wash had lifted the river's face to within a foot or two of the roadway and we seemed to be riding through a flood. The lamps from both brinks were reflected in the river's glistening face and became a glittering black highway with its own strings of lights stretching away into the far distance. The whole town was doubled and made into two places at once.

I was dazzled and made giddy by it, and the feeling did not leave me even when we got to our new home, and my mother, seeing her furniture looking out of place against strange wallpaper, wept again.

She disliked the house from the moment she entered it in 1937, but it was to be her home for forty years, until one night she opened the living-room door and a surge of grey flood water made the carpet rise under her feet. The river had found its way into the town and into her house, and it drove her and my father away for ever.

CONTRASTS

On our first morning in Wisbech we went to look at the river. The glittering highway of the night before had slipped away with the tide, and what remained was a steep-sided channel of mud and brown water. But downstream the high floodbanks made a *V* on the horizon like a gunsight pointing to the Wash, and we were hundreds of miles away from slag heaps and pit-heads and the coal-black Tyne.

It was a bright morning, and I remember the breeze was making a ring of dolphins spin at speed around the golden galleon weather-vane on top of a spire in the centre of town. And the tower had a carillon that rang out a tune on the hour. It wasn't Jarrow.

We three boys, "us lads", soon had to go to school. We were foreigners, and even our accents were a problem.

The first shock, however, was the noise of the southern classrooms. I had been used to silence and folded arms, but now, when a teacher asked a question, the whole class erupted in cries of "Sir, sir!" and jumped about in their seats in a way that would have meant a caning for certain for me at the age of twelve in 1937.

And derision was loud, too. Even a good mark in

an exercise was a hazard. It was Russian roulette. Every number up to ten was safe – except eight. If I got eight out of ten the news would travel round the class and they would wait until I had to call it out to be entered in the register. Then that "eight" would come, but as a straight, flat Geordie "ai-ai-t" and I would be swamped in a great bleat of imitations.

What made matters even worse was that Norman and I, the two eldest, had to go to our father's school. He was the woodwork master and there was no chance of avoiding him. I was in a sweat. What if he called me "Jackie" when he read out the register, and I slipped up and replied "Yes, Dad"!

Neither he nor I mentioned it beforehand – Geordies didn't admit to such mimsy anxieties; there was a code and you were expected to have absorbed it. So we overrode the sniggers with "Gordon" and "Sir" and gritted our way through the lessons like a rigid master and blameless pupil.

The real problems were at home. My mother had had a carefully constructed world in Jarrow, and now it had come tumbling down around her. She came from quite a poor family and tragedy had struck when her mother died. That had led to her being boarded out with an aunt who had married well and lived in one of the posher parts of Jarrow.

The aunt was a ferocious social climber and treated my mother, who was always timid and gentle, as an unpaid servant. She was desperately unhappy, and it was from this that my father, quarrelling with the aunt, had rescued her.

They had scraped together enough to get a mortgage on a new house (which cost £582) and furnish it right down to a rolling pin (ninepence) and an egg beater (sixpence). It meant so much to her that she kept the bills, and I have them now.

Number 124 Wansbeck Road was semi-detached and the road outside was never made up, but she always called that house "a little palace", and when I was born there, a year later, she had a baby to coddle and her life was as full as it could be.

But now she had been exiled and forced to live in a rented house between a canning factory and the gasworks. She never thought she would have to stay there. She always kept a stack of cardboard boxes ready for the removal day that never came, and often she would fall into pits of depression. Without wanting to, she dragged me, more than anybody, down with her. It is one of the privileges of the eldest child.

She tried to make the best of it. Wisbech was always "a clean little town", but it was never "home". In fact Jarrow was home for all of us in spite of what it was like.

It was the time of the Great Depression, the Slump, and I'd seen the Jarrow Marchers set off for London in a last desperate attempt to be given work. But I never did see the cranes in the shipyard working, and the wheels in many pit-heads did not turn, and there was rusting machinery everywhere. Boarded up shopfronts were normal, and so were the groups of men at street corners sitting on their heels, "on their hunkers", pitman fashion. This was all so commonplace that I thought all towns were like that, until we came to Wisbech.

In Jarrow I went to school with boys who were sometimes barefoot, who wiped their noses on the

sleeves of their jerseys because they had never had a
handkerchief, and who ate bread and butter dipped
in sugar and called it dinner. We played together at
school, but outside it was street warfare. One night,
when the old lady next door was dying, I was sent
for the doctor, but once I'd left Wansbeck Road
behind me and the studs on my boots were clatter-
ing under the gas lamps, I was chased from street to
street by gangs of tough lads.

There was nothing wrong with bread and sugar,
or bread and black treacle, we all liked it, but the
poor were marked out. Their backsides hung out of
their trousers and when they were given boots they
had to wear them without socks. Real poverty can
also be an embarrassment to those who are not
suffering from it. There was a gulf, even in Jarrow,
and I knew which side of it I was on.

Beggars would call at our house. They came up
the back lane – what beggar had the right to knock
at the *front* door? Some were ragged men who drank
and were sent away. But there were others.

One day a tall red-headed man came to the back
door. He had his wife with him and she was carrying
a baby wrapped in a shawl. My mother's heart went
out to them and she gave them tea and bread and
butter, but my father would not allow them in the
kitchen. Barriers were barriers. My mother had tears
on her cheeks and she pleaded with him: "Oh, but
the bairn, Norman, the bairn!"

But the man and my father understood each
other; they knew the code.

"No, missus, no," the man said to my mother,
"we'll just squat down out here."

They sat on the kitchen doorstep to eat while I watched. I even remember the way he sat, one foot on the ground and one on the step, like a man taking a break from work. But he had no work, and he offered to sharpen knives to earn what he was given.

My mother found some of our old baby clothes to give to his wife, and my father, who was always a generous man, gave the man some money, but everyone, including me, was shamed.

Wisbech, the clean little town, was different — except to my grandfather. He had worked as a coal hewer in Boldon colliery and as a boilermaker in a Jarrow shipyard, but now he was a tobacconist and had two shops. He was also a Labour councillor, and when he came to visit us in Wisbech his instincts would take him into the back streets. "Why, man," he'd say, "the slums are as bad here as anything in Jarrow."

He was right, but I didn't discover that until much later, when I became a reporter and my job took me into some of those same back streets.

HEADMASTERS

Wisbech Grammar School was just across the road from my father's school but was hidden from it – in more ways than one. It lay behind a high red brick wall and its buildings were old, although not as old as its traditions, which were scholarly and snobbish. It cut the town in two, as it still does, and like all other town kids I'd got used to calling out "Grammar School puppy dog!" whenever I saw anyone with one of those silly caps, quartered in light and dark blue, perched on his head.

And then my father proposed that I should go there. I fought it, but it was no use. I had already passed the exam, and he was to pay the fees. We clashed, and not only over the Grammar School.

My father would never admit that he was stubborn, but in an argument he was about as pliable as a sergeant-major. He wasn't tall, but he held himself as upright as a ramrod, like the soldier he had been in the First World War, and he marched to school.

As a young man he had sung in a church choir, which was hard to believe because he never tired of talking about the pomposity of the clergy and the back-biting of congregations. But in Wisbech we three boys – David, the youngest and by far the gentlest, Norman and I – were packed off to Sunday School at St Peter's Church in the centre of town. And exceptionally dreary it was. Best clothes, Brylcreem as cool as the vicar's clammy hand on your scalp (my father always spoke of him having a handshake like a wet fish), and a penny for the collection.

But then, one Sunday, I exercised my leadership and we got no further than the Market Place. We wandered around for an hour and when we got home I said we'd been too late to go in – which was a mistake, as church is the one place where it's never too late.

My father's anger was great. He had little or no belief in God, unlike my mother, who all her life would go, by herself, to pray among empty pews, but he had a very strong sense of morality. It was like woodwork, a practical matter, and I had offended. Worse, I had led the younger ones astray. He ranted and I was packed off upstairs and had my pocket money docked.

He remained grim. Next week he gave me the choice: "What's it to be – Sunday School or back to your room?"

I went to the staircase.

"Eeh, that boy!" said my mother.

But my father had made his mind up. "That's the end of it, Margaret," he said. "He's a disappointment, but if that's the way he feels I don't want to hear another word."

It was never mentioned again, and we never went back to Sunday School. Normally he was quick to forgive, but this time the gloom had lasted for so long that I think he had realized for the first time that his eldest child, at thirteen, was not really the kind of son he wanted.

At the Grammar School the masters wore gowns, sometimes mortar boards when extra pomp was required, and there were prayers in Latin in the library. The Head had been an oarsman at Cambridge, and oar blades with the names of his crews decorated his study as well as the boarders' dining room.

There must have been boarders, although I never knew one, but I did know their dining room. It lay beyond the green baize door that separated the Headmaster's house from the school. It was there, in the gloom and a smell of cabbage like old farts, that I sat the entrance exam. I was alone because our move from the North had prevented me taking the equivalent of the eleven-plus, so it had been a bit of a struggle for my parents to get me there in the first place.

Once again I was made an alien by my accent, a class marker even more potent than oar blades. (I always wanted to know, but never asked, how the rowers could bring themselves to saw perfectly good oars in half, and did they do *eight* so they could each have one? And what about the cox – did he have half a *boat?*) But I'd never even seen a rowing eight, nor had most of the boys who started school with me that day. We stood in awe of the Great Oarsman.

There was a fat boy called Bill Fovargue. He had a rambling, roundabout way of saying it, but he *liked* the way I talked. He was amused by it, but didn't laugh. Maybe this was because fat boys themselves had a lot to put up with and it was made even worse for him because one of his Christian names was Oberon, king of the fairies, and Bill was far too round to flit anywhere. We became friends.

The Great Oarsman was a tall man with a long head, a face lined like the wrath of God, and wherever he strode the black wings of his gown writhed in the turbulence of his wake.

He was hot on sex – against it, not for it. At prayers one morning he sent the lady teachers packing and then laid into the entire school in a fury. We were gross, we were scum, we had minds "like cesspits". The spittle flew out as he damned us to hell-fire because there were tit and bum drawings on the bog walls and he had just found out. The joy was tremendous.

There were, in fact, much more inspiring drawings on the cubicle doors at the swimming pool where, shivering and shrunken from the muddy river water that filled it, we could read a long poem about the willing habits of a carpenter's daughter.

In any case I had learned far more about sex in my first school in Jarrow. There were kids who knew all the varieties of sexual mechanics, and in fact there's not much to work out, given the small sum of our parts.

The Jarrow headmaster, however, demonstrated more subtle appetites. He had a waxed moustache, a club foot, and he ruled by terror. The echo of his heavy boot on the bare floorboards stiffened your fingers on your pen and made your stomach shrink so much your snake belt became loose. It was the cane for boys, the flat of the hand for girls. If it was a girl he was chastising he would put her head between his knees, lift her dress, pull her knickers tight and slap her behind.

There were no tears in the playground when one morning he fell dead in his bathroom – one last thud and gone.

Wisbech Grammar School was a long way from this. It aped public school with its Houses (purely in the mind and totally without meaning), its Tuck Shop (two trays of doughnuts from Easingwood's café) and its Honours Boards in the library but nobody, as far as I knew, followed the public school vice.

Sex was guilt and a raging interest in girls but, in Wisbech, precious little chance to be with them. There were no girls at the Grammar School; they were across the river in the High School, but even if they'd been next door it wouldn't have done me much good. I was far too shy.

WORDS

Bill Fovargue was always full of good intentions, even though his actions didn't always turn out as he intended. His father was dead and his mother had a little shop in a row of terraced houses on the South Quay close to where the coasters unloaded their timber and grain. She was a large woman and, like Bill, very affable. "Sit your bums down," she'd say as we went into the tiny living room behind the shop.

They had a narrow backyard with a single strip of flowerbed along one wall. It bulged and overflowed with blossoms of every colour and was Mrs Fovargue's pride. One day Bill thought he detected a weed in it and watered it with weedkiller. But he'd used a full packet on the tiny garden, and within an hour the whole border was brown and limp and desolate, and so was Bill when his mother found out.

Mrs Fovargue, who had a large mop of frizzy hair, had a quick temper – as I discovered when I helped Bill take the helmet off a celluloid deep-sea diver, stuff it with sulphur and set fire to it. It was an experiment, because Bill was a scientist before all else, but the diver erupted, set fire to the wash-house window frame and covered the glass with a rash of black spots that never came off.

Why a diver? I've never known. Divers don't catch fire ... but a diver in flames was exactly the kind of sideslip into craziness that would make another friend of mine rub his hands. Not that Treble Smith (his real name was John but he was so wild about music that we'd branded him) was exactly friendly to me at that time. Far from it. He was older than me and lived next door, another one with a widowed mother, and he had a fair claim to being, if not exactly mad, at least very eccentric. We disliked each other at first sight and once, when I was taunting him through a hole in the fence, he threw a knife which quivered in the planks uncomfortably close to me. It wasn't until later that I found we had a lot in common.

Bill was the only slow bowler I knew who believed that the essence of slow bowling was slowness itself. When he ambled up to the wicket, his arm curving over with the grace and speed of a dying swan, you'd see batsmen, ecstatic and dribbling, come forward five paces to pluck fistfuls of juicy runs from him. As a bowler he lasted about as long as I did as a wicket keeper – there was always someone better.

If there was a library at my father's school I don't remember it, but at the Grammar School there was the real thing, a book-lined hall with wooden panels and high windows. I discovered it at just about the time the first of the Penguins was published. In fact it was Penguin No. 1, a book called *Ariel*, that set my mind alight.

It was a biography of Shelley, written by a

Frenchman, André Maurois, and nothing had prepared me for it. For years I'd had a hero, Lawrence
of Arabia, but Shelley, instead of being a furtive
genius, blazed like a comet, scattering atheistic pamphlets, ripping into an unjust society, defying his
father, and perishing in a storm at sea. His body was
recognized only by the book in his pocket, and when
Shelley was cremated on the beach, Byron tore his
heart from the flames. I wanted it – all of it.

Words mattered. I got the first inkling of their
power from one of the mildest teachers I ever knew.
Miss F. K. Moore – I never knew her first name nor
why the whole school called her Magga Moore – wore
her grey hair tied in a bun at the back of her neck,
blushed easily and never raised her voice. But there
was never trouble in her class. A meek, small woman
would stand in front of a gang of boys, cradling a
piece of chalk in her clasped hands, and gradually,
little by little, she'd bring Falstaff out of *Henry IV*,
Part One so that we could see the fat, gross old coward who made her blush deepen.

When I started to write and got things in the
school magazine, she would invite me to tea and we
would talk of Keats and Rupert Brooke. I wrote to
her all the time I was in the Navy, and almost to the
time she died. She knew about words.

I remember the night I got drunk on words. I had
an essay to write for homework and I was, as usual,
reluctant to do it. On top of that it was midsummer
and the subject was snow.

I went to my room, sat on the floor and began to
write. I wrote that the snow lay "like a blanket".
Then I thought again. Snow did, in fact, look like a

blanket, but most blankets were warm, and snow was cold. So I abandoned that and put down that the snow was like a sheet, which was at least white and cold.

It was still not right, but now I was beginning to feel the cold of the snow and could hear my feet crunch in it. But crunch was simply the normal word and it had lost its power. I listened again as my foot broke through the crust and felt it being compacted under the sole of my boot. As the snow was pressed down, the crunch was accompanied by a squeak, and suddenly I saw that I could combine both sounds in one word. I wrote: "the snow creaked underfoot" – and then I saw I had done even more than I knew.

"Creaked" was itself a cold word; doors in empty houses creaked, and an icy wind could make bare, black branches creak. Between crunch and squeak there was a thin gap through which a white land-scape glittered with frost, and creak was the password under the sole of my boot.

I went hunting for words; or rather I charmed them towards me merely by looking and forgetting. I looked at the whiteness and forgot the words that usually clung to it. New ones came, and each one, when it was chosen, seemed to prise open something new about the snow. I couldn't tear myself away from it, and four hours later I was still doing my homework.

TEACHERS

We had a teacher who was a novelist, or rather a novelist who was a teacher because there was no doubt which ranked higher in his mind. John Saint Clair Muriel had the best behaved, most silent classroom in the school. He composed his novels and literary biographies during history lessons, pacing to and fro in front of us, head bowed, breathing heavily into his Rudyard Kipling moustache and glowering through thick, horn-rimmed glasses at anybody who dared break his train of thought.

He also had a bitter tongue which wasn't always directed at us. One expansive day, when he was shredding a few sacred cows for our amusement, he spoke of the Salvation Army "blowing their guts out on the Market Place". But his particular way with words could also land him in trouble. He gave a boy a ten shilling note (worth at least five pounds now) and told him to buy chips with it, by which he meant wood chips for his fire, but "that imbecile went to the fish shop and came back with enough fried potatoes to fill my blasted desk!"

He would sit at his desk writing with a fountain pen filled with violet ink while we silently made

notes from our text books, and then he'd begin his
pacings, looking at the floor, his head deep in the
collar of his suit of ginger tweed. One of us, egged
on by the rest, opened the classroom door behind his
back, and on the return journey he walked straight
out into the corridor. But the expected explosion did
not come – he paced back into the classroom without noticing the excursion.

I knew from the start that my snow essay worked,
but I had it confirmed by a teacher, although not
the novelist. Mr Dimock was a new kind of school-
master to me. He was big and beefy and enthusiastic,
and more interested in bulldozing our brain cells
than standing on his dignity – although Bill
Fovargue could put him to the test.

Mr Dimock lost a book and asked if anyone had
seen it. Bill was always genuinely helpful. He said:

"Was it a green book?" – yes, Fovargue.

"With gold lettering?" – yes.

"About this big?" – that's right, Fovargue, where
is it?

"I don't know, sir. I was just wondering if that's
the book you meant."

The bulldozer provided me with my first audi-
ence. He read the snow essay out to the class and
remained enthusiastic even after Bill, always
hideously honest, called my style "flowery".

After this I began to write at such enormous
length that even Mr Dimock told me to cut back on
the number of pages, but I countered by writing
with a mapping pen and squeezing the words
together.

School was easier, but home was just as difficult.

It was crowded, my mother was only rarely happy, and I had started having rows with my father. He wanted me to obey conventions and "be reasonable", but I was the enemy to all convention and all reasonableness.

Everyone, particularly my father, had short hair; I let mine grow long. In those days it sent out the wrong signals about my sexuality, but I compounded it by wearing green corduroys, and when the order on wearing school ties was reinforced I destroyed mine and wore a white tie with horses' heads.

Then one night in bed I couldn't get my breath and I wasn't the only one who thought I was going to die. It was pneumonia. A new kind of drug pulled me through, but for a long time I lay on my back with time to think.

I had long since discovered that I could hold, without difficulty, two opposites in my mind at the same time. I often dreamt of an object that looked like a cushion but it was both large and small without its size varying a fraction, and in the dream I was continually striving to make other people take in this astounding fact.

And I had always had dreams in which I knew I was dreaming, which was like inhabiting two worlds at once, so that as I lay in bed during those longs days of recuperation I had no real problem in considering myself an atheist who also believed in God.

What made me into an atheist was the age-old problem with Christianity. If God was all-powerful and at the same time benevolent, how was it that there was suffering in the world? The Church seemed to me to give nothing but a feeble and untruthful answer, so I knew what I had to do. I was sweating as though the fever had returned and I was afraid, but I swore at God. The terror of that moment has never grown any less for me – but it was fear of the Church's idea of God that was in my mind, and not God himself. I have gone on believing in the contradictory God who has made opposites into aspects of the same truth – and the best thing about him is that he has seen to it that there are miracles everywhere and we have the imagination to see them.

I wrote a poem that got into the school magazine.

RAIN

Alone in the street,
Rain walks with sweeping strides
Splashing his feet in lonely puddles.
His icicle arrows,
Piercing the air with coolness,
Shatter on the pavement's mirror;
And babbling brooks
Tumble in torrents down dingy drains
To mysteries
That only the Tin Soldier discovered.

At night, roofs flood,
And steadily, sleepily,
Like Time's tapping finger,
Rain drips to the ceiling.

ROOFS

I liked girls, and I was often in love. After infant school the sexes were always segregated – in a big way as far as the Grammar School was concerned because the River Nene lay between us and the girls of the High School on the opposite bank. But there was the bridge between, and all the bans imposed by headmistresses and headmasters could not prevent us mingling there.

As a Geordie boy I had always pretended to have a contempt for "lasses", but I longed for them and was terrified by them ... with some reason. In Jarrow a little blonde had turned me into a shivering weakling when she spotted a rude diagram I had drawn and threatened to tell tales to the Head. But Lucy, when I met her in Wisbech, would never have done that. She was gentle, and at least as shy as I was. She had large eyes in a pale face and she may, she just may, have let me into those female secrets that life had denied me. She was as passionately fond of me as I was of her, but I let her down.

We never even held hands. We cycled around town together, and out into the flat fen countryside, but we never touched. I longed to kiss her, and one

day I made up my mind that I would. Along a lane
we stopped by an orchard gate. We stood, straddling
our bikes, and we talked. I wanted to reach out to
her, and she knew it. But my nerve failed, and I
turned around and rode away.

She followed me and called out my name, but I
rode faster. I saw that she was hurt and bewildered,
but I didn't have the courage to turn back, and we
never spoke again.

I was in a fight at the park gates with a toughie
who was being aggressive to another girl. She
thanked me afterwards, but it led to nothing because
I'd lost the fight and was ashamed I'd quit.

Altogether I had a very low opinion of myself. I
was afraid of just about everything – illness and
germs, fights and girls, and a war was looming up –
not that I noticed that very much; I had too many
troubles of my own.

I thought of running away. I was going to Wales
because I had been swept along by a novel, *Aylwin*,
by Theodore Watts-Dunton, and for a while I
believed I would find some mystical satisfaction on
the slopes of Mount Snowdon as the lovers in his
story had done. I had a route mapped out and I'd
saved some money, but it fell through when I hit on
another way to change myself.

I would resist every temptation and become
monk-like. I took a vow of silence and for weeks I
spoke only when spoken to, and then answered only
in monosyllables. It didn't last; I weakened and
blamed myself for weakening.

In the end there was only one thing for it. I had
to start taking risks or lose my self-esteem for ever.

I walked alone at night and started putting myself to tests.

In Park Avenue, where a girl had been murdered and a cross was cut in a grass plot to mark where it had happened, I would put my back against a tree as a starting point, shut my eyes and set off along the centre of the road regardless of traffic (at night there was very little) and not re-open my eyes until something stopped me or I judged I was at the road's end.

As a variation I would set myself a straight line and follow it over walls and ditches, through paddocks and orchards until I hit a road. I would be miles out in the Fens before I turned back.

I also took to climbing. I went up buildings, alone and at night. The school was easy. The first part was up a drain pipe to a flat roof over a corridor, then a crawl up the tiles of the chemistry lab to the roof ridge. Sitting astride the ridge I would horse my way along to where it joined the old part of the school.

There were window ledges and handholds that got me to the library roof, then it was up the tiles and over the ridge to the other side facing the river. There was a parapet along the front of the school. It was two storeys up and ended with a pinnacle of ornamental stonework over the front door through which only sixth formers were permitted to enter. The parapet was a foot or so wide; wide enough to walk. I did it, and straddled the pinnacle.

Another time I climbed to the wooden belfry at the top of the library and stood on the roof ridge to pin a flag as high as I could reach.

I went up churches, too. At St Peter's I worked my way along the roof leads to a little tower at the end and got inside through an aperture like a doorway. There was a spiral staircase and I felt my way down it until I came to a locked door and could go no further. Next day, from inside the church, I read a notice to say that the door was locked because the tower was unsafe.

But what really caused me trouble was that my jacket and trousers had picked up so much lead oxide from the roof that they were ruined. Once again my father and I were at loggerheads.

STORIES

I was beginning, although I didn't realize it, to store up ideas for stories. A lot of them had to do with water. Inland from the Wash the land lies like a table top floating in the sea, never ever dry and always in danger of dipping completely under whenever the tide laps an inch or two higher. There is a lot of water in the Fens, and the Pingle was a favourite place for suicides.

Pingle Bridge in Upwell crosses the Sixteen Foot, one of the many drainage cuts that keep the Fens above water, and it was to this spot that those in despair would cycle, leave their bikes on the bank, and walk beneath the glassy surface.

I knew what Keats meant when he said he was "half in love with easeful death". I was afraid of death but at times could think of nothing else. I had worked out a monogram on the end-papers of an anthology of verse which made my initials JWG into a skull, and devised a motto in Latin class: *Ubique Mors Est* (Death Is Everywhere). In spite of all this emphasis on mortality the book, battered through being kept in a hammock, survived the Navy.

Bill was a great swimmer and we often used to cycle out and plunge from Pingle Bridge. Unlike the muddy Nene, you could see the green weeds that stroked your limbs and were supposed to wrap round you and hold you to the bottom. It could never happen to Bill, who was as buoyant as a porpoise, but I was skinny and shivered on the bank while he was still placidly paddling to and fro "like a creature native and endued unto that element" – although he was hardly an Ophelia.

I saved a little girl from drowning, but that was in Wisbech where the canal from Upwell ran through the town. It was a stagnant waterway, unused except for skating in winter, and one summer day I was walking home from school along its bank when a shriek went up. A woman was crouching at the water's edge on the opposite side and frantically reaching out to a spot where her daughter had disappeared.

Only the girl's hair showed, spread out on the water beyond her mother's fingertips. I dropped my books, threw off my jacket on the way down the bank and dived. I had the girl out in seconds, and her mother took me into their house on the canalside to dry off. She loaned me a pair of her husband's trousers to give me something dry and later, when the news got into the paper, she called at our house and forced a ten-shilling note on my mother, which I tried to return but it all got too embarrassing so I kept it.

There had been more danger from germs than drowning for either the girl or me, but on two other occasions the water almost got a victim while I was nearby. Wisbech swimming pool was on the riverbank below the town and it was filled from the Nene, which meant that it looked like a vat of cocoa. I hauled a boy out of that when nobody else had realized that he was lying on the bottom and almost dead, and ever afterwards his mother mentioned it whenever she met mine.

The other occasion was more serious. A young boy fell into the river itself. The grass bank was almost vertical at the spot where he'd gone in and he tried to hold on to the piling but couldn't get a grip because of the slime. The current was on the verge of tugging him away when I heard his brother's shout. Once again I saw hair floating on the water but, with someone hanging on to my hand, I got a grip on him. A man hauled him up and pumped him out.

Anybody lost in the Nene could trundle silently through the town, upstream and down, before they surfaced. I saw one who'd done it. A policeman sitting in the stern of a boat held the jacket of the floating corpse and brought it to the steps of the South Quay. The flesh that showed was a cheesy white, and death did not look easeful.

In winter there was skating. I screwed figure skates to the soles of my football boots, but I was never anywhere near as good as the Fen kids who could stay upright for hours without their ankles buckling, and would skate for miles under the moon. Most of them had long since outgrown their first skates, the "Fen runners", which looked like the blade of a table knife set into a block of wood, and had graduated to "Norwegians", which was their name for the high, long racing skates. They outpaced me in every way.

I took heed of their knowledge of ice. They would say, "If she cracks she bears, if she bends she breaks" – which meant that if you heard a cracking sound ringing through the ice it was thick enough to be safe, but if it bent you were going to get wet.

There was an old man in Upwell who, leaving the pub where he spent a lot of his time, would often stagger across the road and straight into a dyke. He would flounder about in the water shouting out, "I'm a swimmer! I'm a swimmer!" until someone hauled him out. But he walked into the water one winter night when there was no one to hear him and they didn't find him until the ice thawed in spring.

He remained submerged in my mind for years before he came to the surface again in a story I wrote called "If She Bends She Breaks".

EVACUEES

The war was a good time for aeroplanes, and I'd always loved them. It began in Jarrow where I'd seen an air circus. Tiny, glittering red biplanes plucked handkerchiefs from the ground with their wingtips or, as green as grasshoppers, skimmed over a car while the pilot leant out of the cockpit and bombed it with flour bags. You could see him, in his flying helmet and goggles, raise his arm and take aim.

For a long time I dreamt of nothing but aeroplanes, and now the air was once again full of beautiful aircraft. There were wasp-waisted Hampden bombers, Lysander reconnaissance planes that were all windows and thin struts like magical flying glasshouses, and Spitfires that spread their almond wings against the sky as if they were married to it.

Spitfires would often come beating down over the rooftops, picking out a single house to impress a girl-friend who lived there, or, out in the Fens, they went scudding under the power lines to impress each other. We stood in the playground and watched one do a victory roll all the way across the town.

A Hampden, a very small bomber, made a forced landing on the North Brink outside town, catching the edge of an orchard and coming to rest in a hedge. Those who got there first found the pilot and his crew sitting on their parachute packs waiting for an RAF truck from the airfield at Sutton Bridge. The bomber was like a great crumpled insect when I got there, and a crowd of souvenir hunters was being chased away, but the smell of petrol and new machinery was the smell of heroism, and I dreamt again of flying.

On a different day, when the clouds hung low and the earth was sodden, the same smell was sickening. A Spitfire, for some reason we never knew, had come diving vertically through the clouds and into a ploughed field. Fen earth is soft and water-logged, and the Spitfire buried itself and its pilot. From the road nothing could be seen except a crane and airmen working in the slippery rain to pick pieces out of the hole.

It was difficult to ignore the war, but I tried — even from the day war broke out. Wisbech took evacuees from London, and on that day I was in my Boy Scout uniform ready to help a trainload of London kids and their mothers find their new homes in the town. It was a sunny Sunday morning and I was in our backyard when I heard Chamberlain's tired old voice on the wireless declaring war on "Herr Hitler".

"Oh, Norman," said my mother, "what's going to happen to the boys?"

"Don't worry, woman," said my father, "it'll all be over before they're old enough to go." Which was a reasonable way to think because I wasn't yet quite fourteen. But on my way to meet the evacuees the air raid siren sounded as I cycled past the gasworks, the only target Wisbech had to offer, and the thought of bombs made me uncomfortable for the first time. I was in uniform, under my wide-brimmed Scout hat, and for once in my life the feeling that I must set an example swept over me, so I made an attempt to cycle *nonchalantly*, which meant weaving about in the road, and I did it so elaborately I fell off.

My mother and father volunteered to provide a home for an evacuee but weren't taken up as our house was already crowded. I helped to round up the mothers and children into groups of about a dozen and as we tramped from door to door I saw how widely human nature could vary.

Many houses made an attempt to take families in as though they were relatives arriving for a holiday, but at others the face that came to the door would cast a very hard eye over our group. Then a finger would point at some nice-looking little boy or girl and a voice would say, "I'll have that one."

But they had no choice, and the billeting officer who was with us would have to argue while the mothers and their children stood by the doorstep and were haggled over. Those were the houses from which the evacuees soon returned to London.

There were big changes at the Grammar School. A whole school, masters and boys, came from London to share our premises. Timetables were rearranged so that we mingled as little as possible with the boys of the Stationers School, but other changes went deeper.

The Great Oarsman had retired and was replaced

by a much milder man; then all the younger men teachers disappeared one by one into the Forces, and were replaced by old men brought out of retirement or young women just out of training college. It was a great opportunity for anarchy. One young lady teacher we sent weeping from the classroom and had to send a delegation to apologize for our behaviour and bring her back before the Head found out. For all his mildness he could lose his rag, as I eventually discovered. But much more typical of what was happening to the staff was a wispy man who was too frail to join up. He was also too frail to teach.

One day he said to the class, "If I were to lie on the floor you would walk all over me." So we did.

The school magazine continued, but now it included a long list of old boys on Active Service, and a lot of the contributions were warlike:

> The Hun, his crosses gleaming,
> Machine guns spitting lead,
> And bomb-racks with their fateful load
> To strike our people dead.

But this piece ended:

> For now the few are many
> And they are hitting back;
> The enemy don't like it –
> But until the gangsters crack –
> They'll keep it up!

A more apprehensive view was in a piece entitled *Satan's Chariots* about bombers, "thin, wicked children of the dark", pointing their "evil snouts" at a town far below, watching the bomb flashes "blossom into little twinkling red and yellow flames" before they turn away "grinning a fiendish grin... A task has been well done by the minions of hell."

The patriotic poem was signed by H. D. Young, and I wrote about Satan's chariots. As it turned out, we were by no means opposites and Dennis and I have grown closer over the years. At that time, however, I didn't know him, or his sister, but she turned out to be very pretty.

ALARMS

I was fifteen and babies horrified me. The smell of talcum powder or of washing drying indoors had always plunged me into misery – another new baby to turn the house upside down and punish me for the sin of just being there. But there hadn't been a baby for years and I thought all that was finished with ... and then, one day I saw a carton of food for "expectant mothers" half hidden on the larder shelf and I realized that my mother was pregnant.

Nobody had mentioned it and I had managed not to see her increasing size, but now the bulge in her pinafore, which I had tried to ignore, was just what I had feared. I kept the guilty knowledge to myself.

This was no way to welcome a brother. I woke up one morning and was told that my mother, taken to a nursing home in the night, had given birth to a baby boy. I pretended it was news but I could not pretend to be happy – unlike another morning soon afterwards when I shouted downstairs to ask what the score was. My father called up, "A hundred and eighty-five for the loss of three of ours." The Battle of Britain and my brother Frank came almost together.

The numbers of planes shot down in the battle were as much a fantasy as Shakespeare's tally of the dead at Agincourt, but I believed them. They helped me to ignore Frank, until one day I saw him very frightened.

We all carried gas masks in little square boxes slung from our shoulders – millions of cardboard boxes had been got ready for the purpose before the war and, although we didn't know it, there were also stockpiles of cardboard coffins – but there were no tiny gas masks for babies. If a gas attack came, babies were to lie in rubber bags with a big window and be supplied with air filtered through a con-certina pump at the side. We had one, but only one attempt was ever made to get Frank buttoned up inside it. He was so terrified that no one ever tried again, and the baby "mask" lay under the stairs for the rest of the war.

But seeing a helpless baby pushing out its bottom lip in real terror worked on me, as it always had in spite of the competition I felt from babies. I could never bear to see the younger ones take risks; any sort of threat to them turned me into a mother hen in an instant (which was something else I had against them), so I would make them cling tight on every fairground ride and would worry if they took on dares. And, as it happened, Frank grew up more like me in almost every respect than the others.

I was jealous of them, yet had to protect them. Not that Norman, two years younger than me, ever needed my protection from anything. He was an extrovert and popular, everybody's idea of what a mischievous little devil should be, unlike me with a load of cares on my shoulders; and David was good-looking and gentle, dark and different to the rest of us, and girls melted for him. Elizabeth, the girl my mother had always wanted, had plenty of admirers and led a girl's life which was foreign to us lads. The Gordons, however, were a clan and we clung together, even though very often I didn't want any part of it.

We were too crowded to have evacuees but my father was not going to be left out of the war. He became an officer in the Army Cadet Force at his school and he was an Air Raid Warden. On top of this he took on evening classes to help keep his family and clerked for a fruit firm in the holidays. When he was at home he was asleep in his chair.

He smoked heavily, rolling his own cigarettes with pipe tobacco, and this and the overwork brought on the TB which, at the end of the war, made him lose a lung and almost killed him.

Sometimes he would take me with him to spend a night at the Air Raid Wardens' post, where we slept fully clothed on camp beds until the sirens sounded. Then there would be telephone calls to report to other posts or we would patrol the streets to make sure no lights showed. The bombers were not interested in Wisbech but we heard the throb of the German planes, quite different to the steady drone of the British and American, as they filed by in the darkness to their targets in the Midlands.

One quiet night, when no siren had sounded and we were lying on our beds, I heard the thump of

explosions and woke my father. We rang around but
nobody had anything to report and I felt foolish. At
dawn, however, we went out exploring and found a
string of craters across a field on the outskirts of
town. No houses had been damaged so nobody had
thought it worthwhile to tell us, but the bombs had
been pretty big judging by the size of the holes.
I slid down into one and it was a perfectly smooth
hemisphere with a little dome of hard, compacted
earth at the very centre. I found a fragment of bomb
case down there.

Not all bombs were so wide of the mark. One
overcast day when we were all at home except Dad
there was a howl in the sky like a diving Spitfire. We
were running out to see it when the howl rose to a
shriek, the air contracted and expanded in a gigan-
tic clap of thunder, there was a split second of
silence and then a rain of bricks and fragments that
punched holes in slates and clattered into gardens.

I tried to make my mother take shelter under
the stairs – a bit late by then, after the bombs had
fallen – but the German bomber, a Junkers, circled
again with its machine gun knocking like a hammer
in the sky.

I went to fetch Dad from his workshop at school.
"We thought we heard a plane," he said. "Did it
drop anything?"

"I'll say it did!" and my indignation made him
and the teacher with him burst out laughing.

The bombs had come down just beyond the end
of our road, aimed at the gasworks, but they missed
the target and the whole stick had fallen along a row
of little houses beside a railway track. We went to

look. One side of the street was jagged heaps of bricks, with rooms suddenly exposed and furniture hanging from upper rooms over piles of rubble. Men clambered over it in the drizzle.

My father helped to search for survivors but only one person was killed, a woman. A man who had been on night shift and was asleep in bed had been blown across the street, still in his bed, and landed unhurt on the roof of a house opposite.

Alongside the railway line lay the leg of a dog. It was there for weeks.

ALL CHANGE

Uncle Frank turned up in Wisbech with a limp. I took him to a Wings for Victory exhibition in the Corn Exchange, and at the RAF display we chatted to a pilot. I was dazzled by the purple and white stripes of the DFC on his breast and I noticed that the top button of his tunic was undone, which was a sign that he flew fighters. He must be a "grand lad", said Uncle Frank, and stumped on with his raincoat and trilby hat looking out of place among all the uniforms. He limped because his leg had been broken when his ship was torpedoed in the Pacific.

He was a solid, broad man with ginger hair and freckles, and soft-spoken to the point of silence. He had been chief engineer on a liner serving as a troop ship, and when it went down his lifeboat had capsized, trapping his leg under the gunwale. Almost all he would tell us about it was that he had lost *forty* tropical suits which he had needed, a newly laundered one every day, for dining with passengers on peacetime cruises.

Uncle Frank, with the kind of reticence that seems to come with long years at sea, played down the glamour of war, and in fact there was very little glamour in it for us. The war seemed to smell of earth. Tall sheets of corrugated iron with a yard of earth between had been erected as blast walls at school and the same structure was used for air raid shelters above ground. We sat in them shivering for hours when there was danger of a daylight raid, and then went for long marches to get warm if fuel had run out and the school had no heating.

Police stations and air raid posts were sandbagged, and every window in every house was criss-crossed with brown paper tape to stop flying glass. The black-out was the greatest danger, and walking through utter darkness one night I held both arms in front of me as I crossed the road but a lamp-post came between them and smacked me in the face. By this time there were a good many people, especially those in authority, who would have gladly done the same.

I had long ago left the Scouts and the school's Army Cadet Corps (although I'd enjoyed marching into brick walls pretending I couldn't hear the orders), and I'd lasted two weeks among the Air Cadets. I was a loner, but I wanted somewhere to go – so I thought of the Communist Party.

I knew a Young Communist, and his revolutionary zeal appealed to me, so I went to a meeting, intending to join. The party met in a room above a shop, but it wasn't there for long because they thought the police were keeping an eye on them, and they were probably right, so they were to flit to a different rendezvous next time.

It was a bare room with a table, a few chairs and a lot of pamphlets, and it was there that I got my first taste of the tedium of politics. They spent endless time debating fine points of doctrine, only once getting down to a practical matter – the smell from the canal which, the chairman maintained, had caused his wife to accuse him of "breaking wind"; he couldn't even use a plain word for that. He was a man with stiff white hair, no humour, and his word was law.

They were suspicious of me, as they would have been of any newcomer, and I saw no place for myself among them so I never went back.

School was more and more difficult. There was talk of expelling me, and my father was summoned for an interview with the Head. He persuaded the school to keep me on and, on the principle that poachers make good gamekeepers, I was made a prefect. I saw through the cunning of that and instantly resigned. The Head, Mr Chesters, made an effort. For half an hour he walked with me, up and down the playground, seeking to change my mind.

"You will be the first one ever to have turned it down," he said – so, of course, I did.

It was 1943, I was seventeen and due to take my Higher School Certificate. I had been working at writing but very little else and there was small chance that I would ever get through, but the war came to my rescue. My call-up papers arrived and I went to Cambridge for my medical. In a series of cubicles the doctors tapped my chest and scrutinized my water and pronounced me fit. Then I was told I could have my call-up delayed so that I could take the exam, but I spurned the chance.

I had been a thorn in the side of Mr Chesters for

a long time, but he got his revenge on the last day
of the Christmas term. During morning assembly
someone near the back of the hall, where we sixth
formers stood, brayed like a donkey and wrecked the
singing of a carol.

When Mr Chesters accused me of being the cul-
prit, which I wasn't, it was beneath my dignity to
deny it, so his last act of term was to order me into
the changing room beside the gym and lash into me
with a cane. I didn't give a damn, but he was a mild
man and the onslaught remained on his conscience.
He wrote to me later, regretting we had parted on
such bad terms – but by Boxing Day I was in the
Navy and my school days were over.

SCAPEGOAT

The Navy began for me on Waterloo Station on Boxing Day 1943. On one of the platforms there was a heap of kitbags and sausage-shaped rolls of canvas lashed with rope – hammocks, though I didn't know it – and they must have lain there a long time for they were filthy with railway grime. Over the years I saw the heap grow until it was a mountain and the canvas at the bottom became as black as coal. It was the lost kit of sailors who had never come back to claim it.

Waterloo was the station for Portsmouth and I was the only civilian in a river of dark blue uniforms that shuffled noiselessly (sailors, unlike soldiers, rarely wear boots) through the barriers and into the carriages where the silence grew deeper. Some kept their black overcoats on, some folded them neatly and stowed them on the racks (sailors take up the minimum of space), and the sleeves of their tight tunics showed badges of ships' propellers or crossed cannons in red or gold. A few of them muttered together for a while and then every single one of them closed his eyes and slept, and the long, smoke-filled compartment rocked silently southwards towards the coast with only me, in my jacket and flannels, keeping watch.

I wasn't to know that on a ship these men were different. Here they were matelots ashore in their "tiddley" uniforms, and the deep U-fronts of their tunics were illegal, as were the wide flares of their bell-bottom trousers which completely hid their buckle shoes. Everything was a mystery to me. They knew something that I didn't, and they weren't saying.

The warm train disgorged us on to the cold platform at Portsmouth – or Pompey in sailor talk – and then I found that in fact there had been a thin scattering of civilians because we were shouted together by a petty officer in gaiters and piled into a lorry. We were the new "draft" for HMS *Collingwood*.

Collingwood was a bleak camp of Nissen huts behind a high mesh fence, but to the Navy it was a ship. A white ensign flew from a tall mast just inside the gate and a painted line marked out the "quarter deck", the stern end of the ship where the flag flew at sea. Whenever you crossed that line you had to peel off a salute to the flag – not that we knew about that yet. We had to struggle to remember that the steel huts did not have floors – they had decks, and the walls were bulkheads, the ceilings were deck heads, windows were ports and corridors were flats. To the Navy, HMS *Collingwood* was at sea, but to matelots she was a "stone frigate".

Within hours I had made my first mistake. The petty officer in charge of our hut asked if anyone had the School Certificate and I admitted it. There was such a sneer of contempt from the thirty others in the hut, all of us still civilians, that I knew, too

late, what I had done. I had branded myself as someone who sucked up to authority. Worse, on the
strength of that admission, without my having any
say in the matter, I was made a "deputy hut leader"
and had to wear an armband.

There was a small gang of Londoners who knew
each other, and to them I was a "college boy", some-
how connected to the ruling classes. My unwanted,
unearned, unmerited armband proved it, and they
decided to make my life hell. They succeeded; my
bed was filled with sand from a fire bucket, kit went
missing, and whenever I made any sort of error there
were howls of public delight. They were a pack and
they were determined to hunt me down.

I stood up to them, but they kept after me so
remorselessly that in the end I gave up and merely
endured. Then I felt, and not for the first time, that
I was a coward. But even that was nothing compared
to the fact that I was so relentlessly disliked. I didn't
know what I had done. Perhaps I was the scapegoat
for all the disgust they felt over what the Navy was
doing to them, but I have never been sure. All I knew
was that the next three months on that landlocked
concrete ship were the most miserable of my life –
and it wasn't the Germans who were responsible.

We were marched from hut to hut for our kit –
mysterious objects such as hammock "nettles", and
jet black scarves called "silks". Every item was sten-
cilled with our names and we were given money belts
to keep our cash close to our bodies because now we
were among thieves.

We sent our civilian clothes home. Shirts seemed
ridiculously soft and effeminate now that we had the

rasp of serge against our skins to dye our elbows and
knees a dark blue. It was a convict's uniform, and
Collingwood was a prison.

But at times there was a painful ecstasy in it. We
paraded at six a.m. in freezing darkness except for a
full moon that made the frost glint and suspended
our breath above our heads like tiny earthbound
clouds. The stars were as sharp as the air that bit our
throats, and the studs of our boots sparked on the
icy roads. I had never seen, been part of, such harsh
beauty.

ESCAPE

At *Collingwood* we were still on the outer edges of the war but occasionally it sent its hot breath our way. I was walking between two rows of huts near the main gate when an aeroplane skimmed the rooftops with its engine coughing. An instant later there was a heavy thump and the air shifted in a great sigh. I ran to the gate and the plane lay just outside, burning in a field. It was one of our own, and this was merely a flying accident, but two men were dead in it.

It was then that I had my first glimpse of how men during the war disguised the shrinking feeling in the stomach that was at that moment making me feel sick. The petty officers on the gate swung it open to allow the emergency trucks through but were not a scrap interested in learning what I had seen, even though the plane had gone right over my head. They watched with a kind of detached curiosity as the fire crews worked their way towards the centre of the inferno and could even, as they talked, smile.

A few months later and I was to see a ship catch fire at night, too far away for my own ship to help because we lay at anchor, and we watched through binoculars as men ran along the deck silhouetted by the flames and the flashes of exploding ammunition. The officer of the watch alongside me, a man who had been at sea all the war, said, "The poor buggers are frying tonight," and went below laughing.

I needed such a pose more against my own companions in the hut than against other dangers, but relief was at hand. I fell ill and was sent to hospital. I had a high temperature and difficulty in breathing, and for a week I lay in bed. It was bliss. I was warm, I was between white sheets and I could sleep all day.

In the next bed there was a tall, lanky, red-headed Scot from the Outer Hebrides. He had a pain in the back and complained that the doctors thought he was shamming. They did, in fact, smile as they spoke to him, but that was because everybody enjoyed his soft Gaelic way of speaking which seemed to turn everything into a story. His home was so far from Portsmouth that he was given three days' travelling time on his leave pass, but he wasn't able to take it up. I was back on the parade ground in a week, still groggy, but he died.

There was a small group of commission candidates at *Collingwood*, and I was one of them. At the end of three months we went before a board where the gold braid asked us if we had been school captains or prefects, and what sports did we play? My answers did not please them – I clearly had no OLQ,

Officer-like Qualities – and I was the only candidate to fail.

The little band showed their pleasure and when, soon after, we put *Collingwood* behind us and went our separate ways they said farewell to the other hut leaders, but not to me.

WALKING ON
WATER

The Navy was very wary of the twentieth century; it was in permanent mourning for Nelson. The black "silk" that we wore was in memory of him. It had to be carefully folded into a long strip, tied in a reef knot under the collar (not sewn, as would have been more sensible, for a knot is more seamanlike) and then draped around the V-neck of the tunic where it was secured by a tape.

I first slept in a hammock, like one of Nelson's men, when I got to Pompey Barracks. In fact Nelson could have walked along one of the mess-decks in the barracks and only the electric light would have been strange to him. The floors were planked and caulked with oakum like the decks of his flagship *Victory*, rows of hooks for hammocks ran the length of the vast rooms, rolled hammocks were stowed in wooden enclosures that ran down the middle, and pot-bellied stoves marked out each mess of about sixty sailors.

The barrack blocks were no more than warehouses packed with men, cargo to be sent out piecemeal when a warship needed them. Hundreds lived on each floor in the same huge room, and there were three floors to each of the barrack blocks.

In spite of all the space the overcrowding was so bad that there were never enough hammock hooks, but I managed to get a place that first night. The "nettles" of a hammock are the fans of strings that hold up each end of the canvas, and I soon learned that I also needed a "stretcher", a length of wood to keep the nettles spread out and prevent the hammock folding itself into a tube and encasing you like a chrysalis.

Once it is slung a hammock is quite comfortable, and certainly better than being spread out on the deck, for a hammock mattress (made of canvas, of course) is very short and you only have one blanket. If you did have to sleep on the floor or a table you had to be the first to clear away your gear in the morning, and then you had the hazard while you were eating your breakfast of having the horny foot of a matelot from the hammock above coming down into the butter.

The piled messdecks were a warren (there were reputed to be men who came into barracks once a fortnight to draw their pay and then vanished until next pay day) but I lost track for ever of all members of the little band, and I had learned never to volunteer for anything ever again.

A ship did not come quickly. I was drafted to a working party in Portsmouth Dockyard to help the civilian riggers who manoeuvred ships in the basin. Every quayside was jammed with ships because the invasion of Europe, the "Second Front" that was chalked up everywhere, was not far away. Landing craft were tied up two or three abreast, and some of them already had very strange cargoes – their decks were jammed solid with row after row of rocket racks for attacking the shore.

An even odder sight was to see a man walking on water. It was flat calm, there was no vessel within hundreds of yards of him, but he stood on the surface and slid along. He came closer, and then I saw he was clinging to a periscope. He came right alongside the jetty on which I stood, and a crane lifted his miniature submarine out of the water and put it on a railway truck.

Flying bombs came over, often at dusk. We were billeted in a church hall in the city and whenever the siren went we would go out into the street to watch these buzzbombs – until one evening we got a very good view of one as it came throbbing low over the chimney pots. Its engine cut, and we dived below ground faster than it did.

Now I was with men who had been to sea, and the little band was far away. We "went ashore" together, although this only meant walking down the road, and I began to discover Pompey pubs. They were crowded to the door, every one, as pubs always were during the war, hot and thick with smoke, and girls arguing about their price with matelots in the corner.

There was an Irishman who claimed to have had the wheel of his bike shot out by English troops when he was a boy – "and I was only going for a penny for the gas," he said, and we imitated his accent so that "ponny for the goss" became a watchword along the dockyard jetties. We had a Liverpudlian who made everything funny, even at breakfast time, in broad Scouse: "It's kippers and custard again."

One who joined in very little was a thin man with
pale and expressionless eyes. He said almost nothing,
but he let it be known that he had razor blades sewn
into the rim of his cap which he could use like a
scythe in a pub fight. He would stand on the outskirts of the illegal gambling schools which operated
behind the dockyard buildings, watching but never
joining in, unlike Geordie, who was the only
Tynesider apart from myself.

Geordie must have been about forty but had led
a tough life and looked a lot older. He was not tall
but he was pure muscle, even in the brain. He had
been a fairground boxer and a lot of his teeth had
gone, both ears were screwed up, and his nose was
so flattened that his nostrils pointed forward. There
seemed to be no depravity he hadn't taken part in
and I enjoyed listening to him, but he was punch
drunk, so far gone as to slur his words and repeat
himself. He lost his money at Fan Tan or Crown and
Anchor and would snuffle about the billet like a
gorilla, tame but touchy, until next pay day.

On night duty in the dockyard we slept where we
could in a sail loft that was still part of Nelson's
Navy. It had a huge cutting floor where canvas for
sails was laid out and there was the heady scent of
hemp and tar. It was close to the riggers' workshop
where we spent our days, and I was good with ropes
so I enjoyed splicing hawsers between calls to the
dockside where we tied up ships or cast them off
when they sailed.

Then, in what seemed like a single night, the harbour emptied. The grey ships slipped their moorings
and left nothing behind but empty jetties and the

smell of oil. Nothing stirred in the Solent, and it was as though the war had packed up and gone somewhere else. Which it had, because the invasion of Normandy had begun.

Next morning the war came back, but quietly, almost peacefully. Ambulances, all empty, rolled through the gates and parked themselves in silent rows on the jetties. Then mobile canteens turned up and we lounged against the bollards smoking our Duty Frees and drinking tea.

For hours nothing happened, and then a large vessel came gliding in. It was a Tank Landing Ship with tall doors in its bows. It nudged alongside and we caught the heaving lines thrown down to us and hauled the hawsers to the bollards as she tied up. Then the first row of the ambulances edged forward.

The ship had served a double purpose. It had delivered its tanks to the beaches, and now it was bringing back the wounded. There were racks of stretchers in its tank bays, and they were carried down two gangways and into the ambulances. There was no noise. The soldiers lay silently under grey blankets with here and there a stab of white bandage. Some were asleep or unconscious, others were looking for a smoke. They did not cry out or moan.

Some were walking wounded and appeared to be untouched. I remember one in particular. He smiled apologetically as he came down the gangway, as though he had no right to be there, and when he got to the jetty he sat on a bollard, insisting that the stretchers should go ahead of him. I fetched him a cup of tea and he took it, but as he raised it to his mouth his hand jerked and trembled too much to allow him to drink. He put both hands to it, but he still couldn't get it to his lips so I held it for him. "Sorry," he kept saying. "Sorry."

The whole operation was very efficient: outward bound with a cargo of tanks; a cargo of damaged men by return.

The next day, at the same quayside, we tied up the battleship *Warspite*. It was a drifting hill of armament, its huge fourteen-inch guns smoke-blackened from firing, and empty cartridge cases from smaller guns were stacked on its decks. And from it came the whistling hum that I had heard from other ships, but this time louder and surrounding it like a force field that would be dangerous to touch.

It had been in action and some of its crew, standing in little knots on outcrops of the grey hill, waved and cheered at us on the quay below. I felt the thrill of it, but the old sailors with me did not wave back. Bombarding a coastline from miles out at sea was not their idea of heroism.

There are not enough men in the crew of an Infantry Landing Craft to do any cheering, and there was nobody on the jetty to see them when they tied up with their sides punctured by gunfire. One had a shell-hole right through its main deck with earth splashed around to cover the blood.

WHALE ISLAND

An aircraft carrier, holed below the water-line by a torpedo, was edged slowly into dry dock. Scrambling nets had been secured over the hole to prevent whatever was inside from floating out during her voyage home but, as the water in the dock was pumped out and more of the hole was revealed, an appalling stench drifted over the dockyard. There had been men in there.

Teams of sailors wearing face masks, rubber boots, and gloves to their elbows went in to take out the bodies, and a morgue was improvised in a shed. The carrier was in dock for weeks, but the smell was still lingering when I was drafted again.

The gunnery school at Whale Island was reckoned to be the toughest place in the Navy. Discipline was fierce. Halfway across the bridge that connected it to the mainland in Portsmouth Harbour the new draft was given the order to Double March. Matelot fashion, we broke into a shambling trot. The bark of a warrant officer cracked across our backs and whipped us into a run that never, from that moment, stopped. We ran to meals, to lecture rooms, and more than once to purser's stores to replace the parts of our uniforms that we had illegally altered.

Hidden away in little shops and houses in Pompey back streets there were tailors who would put gussets into trousers to double the flare of bell-bottoms, cut away the V front of a tunic to a deep U or even, for some really "tiddley Jack", make the tunic so skin tight that the only way of getting into it was to have a zip from armpit to waist. Black-gaitered, black-browed gunnery instructors snarled us all back into once more looking like the newest of recruits. It was a come-down.

Naval gunnery is a pernickety art, having to deal in fractions of degrees if a shell is to land anywhere near a target miles away, and made doubly difficult because the gun platform itself is heaving with the ship. Which must be why the parade ground was at the centre of everything on Whale Island. It was a question of precision, and they drilled us like Guardsmen.

Full-size guns were housed in sheds and we aimed and fired them at tiny moving targets like the ducks in a fairground shooting gallery. The shells, however, were the feathered darts of air rifles mounted on top of the real gun barrels.

An attempt was made to give us a taste of the real thing by closing us up to a gun in pitch black darkness, and having us load and fire and aim while the deck heaved on rollers, water gushed down over our oilskins, and smoke and flashes and noise roared around us. All this was Disneyland, and not in the least as frightening as a genuine practice shoot on a calm day – as I was soon to find out.

To round off our training we were sent north and I went to sea for the first time. At Lamlash on the

Isle of Arran we boarded an old cruiser. The sea rolled with an oily smoothness and our ship swayed with it in the rain as we gazed at the receding shore like wistful emigrants. But there was the business of guns to take our minds off it.

The shells of a gun with a six-inch calibre weigh exactly one hundred pounds and have to be ram-rod-ded into the breach before the bags of cordite are put in and the breach-block closed. We watched it done, and waited for the gun-layer to pull the trigger. The gun went off with a giant's cough that sent out a sheet of flame, a blast of heat and a roar that lifted our feet off the deck. The recoil sent the barrel back with a punch like a car smash. And all of this was engineered to kill someone – ourselves, most likely.

There seemed to be as much danger behind as in front of the gun, and there was more than one of them going off together. Running to grab the next shell from the ammunition hoist beneath the muzzle of the gun next door on its raised platform seemed the height of folly. Cordite came up in a leather carrying case, and as likely as not it would fly open and expose the red bag of gunpowder which needed only a spark to set the whole thing off. And at that moment the gun just above you would belch a great dragon of flame and send its heat licking around you. It was very worrying.

Under the breach of each gun was a large wooden tub such as Nelson's gunners would have used, and its purpose was the same. The rammer was dipped into the tub between each shot to swab out any burn-ing fragments before the next cordite bag was pushed in. Hugging a one hundred-pound shell, I was just getting it to the breach when the ship gave a slow lurch, I lost my footing, the shell fell on the edge of the tub and turned it right over. The shell went rolling away down the deck with me trotting after with a cascade of water splashing around my ankles.

It got worse than that. The target on the horizon was an enormous lattice-work square on a barge being towed on a very long hawser by a tug. When it came to my turn to aim the gun at the target I was squinting down the telescope and was just about to pull the large brass trigger on the handle when the petty officer hauled me away.

"A word in your shell-like ear, my son," he said. "You've got this frigging cannon aimed right at the frigging tug!"

I gazed over the side and could have laid myself to rest in the oily waves, but at the end of it all I had a badge on my arm, a gun with a single star, and I was posted back to barracks to await a draft that might, at last, mean a ship.

FOAM

I didn't need a hammock on my first ship because it had been built in America. HMS *Foam* was a minesweeper loaned to the Royal Navy for the duration of the war, and she was well ahead of British ships when it came to comforts for the lower deck. So we slept in three-tier bunks with sprung mattresses, and the messdeck was arranged cafeteria fashion. The Admiralty, however, had set its weather-beaten face against the washing machines built into her and they had been removed. We hearts of oak continued to dhobi our clothes in buckets in the Nelson tradition.

I joined *Foam* in Harwich. She was tied up in Parkeston Quay and I had to clamber over several other ships to get my kitbag and hammock aboard. I was the replacement for a gunner who had been drafted and I was directed to his bunk – or that's what they told me, because only the greenest of the green would have chosen that particular billet on a minesweeper.

The most important thing about a minesweeper is that there's not much of it below the water-line; you don't want your bottom deep enough to touch off the horns of any mine that's down there. *Foam* was one of the larger class of sweepers but even then she drew only eight feet of water so, despite her size, she floated like a cork – and that meant she rolled.

We had been at sea only an hour when, coming to a doorway that faced the ship's side, I saw no horizon; there was nothing but water from top to bottom of the opening. A second or so later and there was nothing but sky. And then I realized I was holding my balance on an enormous swingboat, pointing first towards heaven and then down into the hoggin, which was what I was learning to call the sea.

Foam, however, didn't roll so much as she corkscrewed, with the odd attempt at a somersault. There was a pendulum in the wheelhouse that often showed us rolling more than forty degrees either way, far enough to show the asdic dome (used for detecting submarines) on our keel – as we knew from watching our sister ships in the flotilla.

That night I discovered why my bunk was not in the choicest position. My weight suddenly increased so that I pressed deep into the mattress. I was so heavy that even breathing seemed difficult. But a moment later I became as light as an astronaut and very nearly floated free. The bunk fell away beneath me and I guessed what was happening. I was being flipped up and down like a tossed pancake simply because I was right against the ship's side, where the rise and fall of the roll was at its greatest. And alongside my head, on the other side of the plating, I heard the water rush and recede as we ploughed through the night.

Minesweepers were no place for anyone who suffered from seasickness. I was still an Ordinary

Seaman, the lowest rank possible, but I soon found out that I could stand being bucked about better than many old sailors. In fact I enjoyed being at sea. I liked to see *Foam* dip her gunwales under, sluicing her decks with green, or push her head into a trough so that white spray thudded and lashed at her superstructure. So immune was I to seasickness that in the messdeck I could watch as other people ran for the side while I carried on eating.

I was quite at home with anything to do with seamanship. I knew my knots and hitches, and understood anchor work and tying up to buoys, I could climb, and I could steer a ship and keep her on course. I didn't care where I was so long as it wasn't in barracks.

The flotilla swept for three sorts of mine at once. We towed orepesa floats, shaped like torpedoes, which held a cable out from the ship's side to cut through the moorings of contact mines, and at the same time we floated a long length of electric cable astern to set up a magnetic field and explode magnetic mines. Under our keel we slung a large metal drum with an electric hammer rapping away inside it to throw sound waves ahead of us through the water and set off any acoustic mines lying on the bottom.

Trailing all this gear, we spent long days sweeping the shipping lanes, keeping station on the other sweepers to clear as wide a channel as possible. It was surprising how rarely, when a floating mine bobbed to the surface, that gunfire exploded it. They were mostly punctured and sank, but the other types of mine were meant to be set off where they lay.

I was in the mess one day when a sudden thunderous shock put out all the lights, and I ran out to see the sea boiling just astern. A magnetic mine had gone off practically under our tail, which was not according to plan. On another occasion the ping of the asdic picked up a submarine and we ran to action stations. Apart from light armament, we had only a single three-inch gun forward and my position was gun-layer so I sat at the handles ready to train the gun at a conning-tower. I was scared, but very conscious that the tin hat wobbling on my head was pretty useless up there. If we were going to be torpedoed the hat would have been of more use under my backside. However, if there was a sub, it got away.

On some clear days we saw the trails of the German V2 rockets, vertical white columns, standing up from the French coast. They were beautiful to see, stretching up to heaven, but somewhere in London they had already dug their huge graves.

We anchored at night and once, when I was on anchor watch, I saw a flash on the horizon and then flames. They spread out and then my mate and I saw it was a ship. I went below and called out the officer of the watch. Through our binoculars we watched men, silhouetted by the flames, flickering to and fro while ammunition made blue flashes like fireworks. Whether the ship sank I never knew, but gradually the flames diminished and the officer, grunting about "frying tonight", went back to his bunk.

It was from the *Foam* that I fell overboard while we were in harbour, but I wasn't the only one to get wet in Harwich. I went ashore with a shipmate and in a crowded cinema we climbed over the backs of our seats to get out. We were in the back row upstairs and we found ourselves on a ledge which, matelot fashion, we walked along. The trouble was that, in the darkness, we knocked over a fire extinguisher and it went off. My mate picked it up and caused instant indoor rainfall.

"Put it down!" I said. He laid it flat, but then the jet rattled along the necks of the back row like a stick against railings. We could still hear the hissing and swearing from the foyer, but we vanished into the black-out.

Soon after this I was drafted back to barracks.

HUNT CLASS

There was a fox's head in the wardroom of HMS *Stevenstone*. She was a Hunt class destroyer and the trophy had been presented by the Stevenstone hunt in the West Country. Recently I came across the same fox's head in a pub in Devon, but I first saw it in London's dockland where the *Stevenstone* was recommissioning. Her bows had been holed by a mine in the North Sea – we didn't manage to sweep them all – but she had been repaired and was on her way to the war in the Pacific.

Destroyers, unlike minesweepers, are built for speed. *Stevenstone* was slim, with a low waist, and she bit into the water with her sharp bows. I was in the after messdeck, close to the waterline again, but the *Stevenstone* was British and we slept in hammocks lashed so close they touched. At night, coming down from the upper deck, you had to stoop under a solid roof of sagging hammocks all swaying, pausing and reversing in perfect harmony.

A hammock is convenient and comfortable as long as you sling it high enough – slung loosely, and you sleep bent up like a safety pin as well as getting continually thumped and sworn at from below. Hammocks even have their uses when they are lashed up like canvas-covered sausages because they can be used to plug the gap if the ship is holed, and *Stevenstone* had already used hammocks in this way. My hammock was also my library and my *New Anthology of Modern Verse* is still soft and bent from its place under my mattress.

There's never space on a warship; the crew has to fit around the machinery, and so ammunition hoists penetrate messdecks and you are certain to have a cannon on the roof. In the fo'c'sle you will also have the anchor chain over your head and the chain locker next door, but I had quickly learned the sailor's trick of sleeping whenever I could, and when I was billeted forward I was able to remain unconscious when we dropped anchor and the chain ran out through the hawse-pipe like the Devil's drum.

Nobody sleeps when a four-inch gun goes off, however. They give a more savage bark than the roar of a six-inch, and then there's the clatter as the brass cartridge case flies out and hits the deck. On *Stevenstone* we did a lot of practice shoots on sea trials. Learning to keep clear of flying cartridge cases, several pounds of hurtling brass, always seemed more important than anything else.

It is possible to see a shell just after it is fired. If you stand directly behind the gun, the shell's base shows as a shimmering disc as it disappears into the sky. Then, much later, you spot the spout of water where it lands – and then another and another as it skips over the ocean.

Destroyers have a deeper draught than minesweepers and ride the sea in a different way. When, at last, we left England we hit a storm in the

Bay of Biscay and you could feel *Stevenstone* slice her way into a wave, parting the waters, but in the end having to yield to a greater force and ride up. Then, still churning away astern but with her bows over the trough, she would slide down and push her snout into the next wall of water.

Aft of the bridge, a destroyer's deck lies close to the water and in bad weather she is often awash. In the Bay of Biscay I saw for the first time wires rigged with sliding toggles for anyone to cling to as they made their way along the upper deck.

And then, one morning, I came up from below and the war seemed to be over. It had slid away with the storm and the grey-green sea was blue, a deep violet blue like peacock feathers, and it was slipping along our flanks in long, voluptuous slopes and hollows. The English coastline, wrapped in fog and rain and war, had long since disappeared and now, on the horizon, there was a line of hills baking in a sun so hot it had forced them into a chemical change and they were bright orange. It was sudden, like walking on to a stage and feeling the heat of the footlights, and the sea was dotted with the brilliantly painted boats of Portuguese fishermen.

A big picture book had opened and the world had changed. Even Gibraltar could not take away the glamour of the Mediterranean, although it did its best. It was English, with policemen and football pitches, and although there were melons in the shops, every café advertised fish and chips. It was like Portsmouth with sunshine, and I wandered about on my first shore leave in a foreign port knowing there had to be something better than this.

RED SEA

Our voyage to the Pacific was interrupted. We were in Malta when we first heard of a bomb with a new kind of explosive that had been dropped on Japan. It was just a bomb; some kind of weapons development such as the "proximity fuses" that were being fitted to the shells we fired so that, miraculously, they went off when they passed close to the target.

A proximity fuse was a nose cone of green plastic and was semi-transparent so that you could see some of the mechanism inside, weird and dangerous. At first, the atomic bomb seemed no more than a device such as that, but soon we learned more about it. Then I wondered why it was necessary to drop it on a *city*, and I got into arguments. Couldn't it have been demonstrated to the Japanese on an island somewhere? I said, but I was shouted down. The bomb had ended the war in the Pacific, hadn't it? – so it was a case of "hoist the gangway, I'm inboard" because now I was never going to be shot at.

Not quite right, as it turned out, and I had a nasty moment with a proximity fuse, too.

During firing practice one of my mates on the gun

crew dropped a shell near my feet and the plastic cone broke off.

°"What should I do?" He had the jitters, and wasn't alone.

"Chuck it over the side!" I said, and I grabbed the shell and flung it after the fuse. I got a rollicking, but nothing was going to make me hug a shell that was perhaps silently ticking.

In Malta, the superstructures of bombed and sunken ships still showed above water in Grand Harbour, but now it was peacetime and *Stevenstone* prepared for a cruise in the Red Sea.

Old sailors' stories had told us that all ports in the Middle East stank, but the smell that drifted towards us from Alexandria was hot and dusty, and seemed to me to have the desert in it.

Beggars slept in the streets. Their rags were worn to such a mesh of gossamer that many layers were needed as a covering and every shred was sun-scoured to the same dun colour. At dusk, each lay like a chrysalis on the pavement and we, in our white ducks, picked our way among them. And if they were ill they died. To look at a photograph taken at that time you can be certain that every dog or horse in the street is long since dead; and every beggar, too.

Do not, we were advised, hand money to beggars, but how can you refuse when a heap of rags is pulled aside to reveal a monstrous swelling where there should have been a limb? So I did so, in a Cairo street, and learnt what the warning was about. Within seconds I was in the middle of a thorn bush of brown and grasping fingers. It was threatening, and I pushed my way through and ran.

And we had to learn we were unpopular simply because we were British. I found it difficult although, having been shouted at as a "Grammar School puppy dog", I should have known better. Shoeshine boys would threaten to throw polish on your white uniform if you ignored them, and I saw a very tall man striding along, barefoot and arrogant, pick fleas from his rags and flick them our way.

There was a huge gulf, but it did not prevent us trading. Piastres bought packets of postcards you would never show your mother, but you could buy her a leather purse embossed with the pyramids. There was even a trade in tiny bottles of "Spanish Fly", reputed to be an irresistible aphrodisiac, but it had such an appalling reek that it must have been the world's greatest turn-off and I never heard of anybody trying it out.

The ship made hardly a ripple as it passed through the Suez Canal, propellers barely turning so as not to wash the sand from the banks, and once we were out into the Red Sea the heat seemed to paste us to the ocean. We rigged canvas awnings that made the upper decks into open-sided tents, but the heat was still so ferocious that I saw a stoker come up from the engine room sweating so much that the thick soles of his boots left wet footprints.

The Red Sea, however, was blue – Arabian blue, which is hot – and everything was as sharp-edged as a jewel. Flying fish, fleeing ahead of us, lifted from our bow wave like glittering brooches, the white spout of a whale etched itself on the blue, and when we were at anchor the clear water beneath our keel was ornamented with all shapes and colours of fish.

The same hard edges existed among people; there was no compromise between rich and poor. Even in Malta the gash buckets on the messdecks where we threw our waste were sorted through by boatmen for edible scraps and usable tins, but when we sailed into Jeddah on the Arabian coast there was keener poverty than that. Women, shrouded totally in black, crouched on the quayside sweeping up the scanty spillage from a cargo of corn and separating it grain by grain from the dust and sand.

Black for women, white for men – and whitest of all for men of wealth and power. In the crowded street of the market we were looked on as something strange, but no beggars pestered us. There was not much noise, and even less when a man with a face like a hawk, fierce and contemptuous, came striding through. He was dressed in robes of dazzling white from head to ankle, black cords around his head-dress, and he was cutting the air at his side with a short whip. He did not deviate his track by an inch nor slow his pace, and the crowds parted ahead of him.

In harbour we flew the Arabian flag, green with a silver scimitar. The scimitar meant what it said – here we were under the rule of the sword.

I was one of the guard of honour when an Arabian prince came aboard. We presented arms while a cannon directly over our heads cracked off a salute that jumped our feet from the scorching deck, but we were toy soldiers compared to the bodyguards that accompanied him. Their black eyes stared everyone down, they had curved knives in their belts, bandoliers over their shoulders and they carried rifles.

There was no doubt that they would use them. Two went with the prince to the wardroom, but two remained in the boat alongside, sitting in the full glare of the sun and watching every move that anyone made.

SHORE LEAVE

Stevenstone must have had more money aboard her than any ship in the Mediterranean Fleet. We had loaded it under guard in the East India Docks in London, crate after crate of it, and the heaviest loads I ever shifted. It was new currency, minted in England and destined for some Middle Eastern country. It had been stowed in the tiller flat, the compartment at the stern that housed the steering gear, and a guard had been posted on it even at sea.

Sweating to unload it, we were cheap labour at twenty-six shillings a week but richer by far than the men in dug-out canoes who came alongside us when *Stevenstone* went "showing the flag" at tiny ports along the coast of the Sudan and Eritrea. They dived for coins, but I never saw any of them go as deep as an old man who went after a tea mug that one of my messmates dropped overboard. It was almost out of sight before he slid from his dug-out, and he himself went so far down he vanished, but he got it.

At Port Sudan we showed silent Charlie Chaplin films to equally silent crowds of men and boys squatting on the jetty, and one night, riding at anchor offshore, *Stevenstone* gave a firework display. Duty watch was provided with hand-held lifeboat flares and lined the ship's side, setting them off and waving them in a circle – which meant that those of us on the seaward side put on a show for the empty ocean.

Rockets went up from the bridge and we fired star shell. Guns make a duller thump when firing star shell because they need only a reduced charge to hoist them into the sky, but once up there they hang incandescently from their parachutes, dripping white fire and shedding a ghastly light.

Shore leave in the Red Sea was never riotous. There were no dives such as those in "The Gut" in Malta where I lost a tooth in a punch-up and spent a night in a cell. Instead we were taken to a rest camp in the hills where there was decorous roller-skating and not much else. Not on the camp, at least. Just outside the perimeter, so that nobody could claim it to be part of the establishment, was a brothel.

It was a wooden, single-storey shack with a roof of corrugated iron. Inside, instead of the bead curtains and soft lights of Beirut where you could sit and drink as in any café, there was a square open space from which doors led to tiny rooms. The girls were black. Several of them were eating, squatting on the floor around a dish, and one or two sat on the beds in their rooms. None of them was very tall – how old they were I don't know – but any of them, haggling only a little, would go with any sailor to her room and the door would close.

Strange place for a schoolboy; terrifying place for a girl. I don't remember how much they charged. I had money in my belt, but I could not look steadily at a girl and calculate her worth against the scale of my desire. Or rather I could, because they *were* pretty and they *were* available, but it shamed me to show it. Where was love? I thought sex was love. I went out. But those girls stayed there, penned like animals.

ORION

The only time I ever came under fire was in the Mediterranean. I had left *Stevenstone* in Malta, had a short spell in a barracks which was converted from an ancient prison but was still more comfortable than Portsmouth, and joined a much bigger ship.

HMS *Orion* was a cruiser, but for me it was a barracks afloat and I could have been back in Pompey – bugle calls and parades, and it was so crowded I had to sling my hammock in a corridor (a flat, in Navy terms) under a fan shaft where I could hear the rats scuttling. I had just climbed in one night when something soft and furry brushed against my naked back. I leapt out ... and the ship's cat came with me, but after that I always stuffed a sock into the vent above my head.

My action station for the first time was in a fully enclosed gun turret that housed a pair of six-inch guns. At least it was enclosed for all the crew except the two gun-layers who sat between the guns with the sighting ports open. We plugged our ears with cotton wool, but when the order "Shoot!" came and then the "ping-ping" of the warning bell, life became for a second one obliterating roar of flame and smoke.

Corfu is one of the most beautiful islands in the Mediterranean, and *Orion* went there with the cruiser *Superb* on a "showing the flag" mission. On a bright morning we were sailing through the channel that separates Corfu from the Albanian mainland, the white ensigns standing out from our mastheads, when someone spotted a puff of smoke on the grey cliffs of Albania. A few seconds later a shell made a waterspout astern of *Superb*, and then more shells came, falling on both sides of us.

I was scrubbing the quarterdeck and, like everyone else, I took shelter behind a turret to the lee of where the shells were coming from. When I peered around the edge I saw the puffs of smoke and tried to gauge where the next shell would land. No action stations sounded, but I thought I'd better get to my gun so I ran forward – on the sheltered side – and began clearing it away, opening the ports and gripping the handles ready to train a pair of cannons on the cliffs.

I really wanted to do it, my blood was up and I longed to blast those shore guns out of existence. It was entirely different to that grey day in the North Sea when I sat at my gun and was so afraid I could feel the tin hat wobbling on my head. Perhaps wars should be fought only on fine days. But my blood lust was disappointed for we got out of there at full speed, and the dozen or so shells fired at us all missed.

It was the beginning of the "Corfu Incident". Albania, an unfriendly dictatorship, claimed that the cruisers had been sailing through territorial waters. In fact, this was impossible as we had been forced to keep to a recently swept channel through a wartime minefield and it was a waterway open to all shipping.

There were protests, of course, and that could
have been the end of it except that a few months
later, in the same stretch of water, two of our
destroyers hit mines that the Albanians had secretly
laid in the swept channel and told no one. Forty-four
sailors were killed. Not a great deal got into the
papers in England, but every sailor in the
Mediterranean Fleet knew that those men had been
murdered. One of them, I learned later, had joined
the Navy when I did and had trained with me at
Fareham.

By this time I had left *Orion* and was once again
on a destroyer, the *Chevron*, and happy to be on
small ships again. However, the Corfu Incident came
close once more when one of the damaged destroyers, the *Volage*, lay alongside us in Malta. Her bows
had been blown off and the ragged and twisted metal
showed where six men had died. They were never
found.

Our flotilla patrolled the coast of Palestine to stop
small boats from landing illegal immigrants. It was
unheroic work and nobody felt happy when at night
our searchlights would pick up a little caique and
we'd have to send a boarding party to it. The people
crowded into the caiques had been persecuted
already, and now we were being used to blight their
hopes once more.

We escorted a prison ship with drab crowds of
refugees penned behind barbed wire on the upper
deck. It was a ghetto afloat. *Chevron*, as if showing
off, cut dazzling circles around her, but our pranc-
ing had its comeuppance.

When a destroyer turns sharply at high speed,

even in a flat calm, she can heel over until her upper deck dips under. *Chevron*'s did so and, in the after messdeck, we had put out wind scoops to get a cool breeze. Instead of air, they scooped sea. Solid columns of water shot clean across the mess with the roar of a waterfall and drowned hammocks, lockers and us. I thought we were sinking, and we bailed with buckets.

MATELOT

Being a sailor was fine. I didn't enjoy guns but I wasn't afraid of the sea – or not very. I thought I wasn't bad at being a seaman, ordinary or not, but the sea is never placid for long and you are never its master. So, on *Chevron*, I was seasick for the first time. I had been on my back for a week with sandfly fever and I'd got to my feet just as we left Alexandria. There was the slightest of swells but I had to hang over the rail with the other unfortunates, some of whom had to do it every time we left harbour. Nelson was the same.

I quite enjoyed a storm, and when *Chevron* was butting her head into the waves I volunteered to venture on to the fo'c'sle with a lifeline around my waist to secure a loose shackle. But this was the kind of bravado that had made me overreach myself aboard the *Orion* one night.

I had taken the place of a messmate who had to climb to the crow's-nest but didn't like heights. A gale was blowing and *Orion* was rolling, but climbing within the shelter of the bridge was no problem. Once above that, however, the wind and spray clutched at my duffel coat, and the mast cut a wider and wider arc against the black sky the higher I

went. I began to get worried, and when I reached
the yardarm I realized what I had let myself in for.
The yard was massive, like an overhanging cliff, and
I had to tilt backwards to clamber over it before I
could work my way to the front of the mast and
drop into the narrow little tub. And I had to do it
as the man I was replacing climbed out.

Naked fear had me swearing at the top of my
voice, into the wind, at the flat caps of the officers I
could see in the safety of the bridge far below. I had
to make the climb twice during the night, but I was
there at dawn when the wind had dropped, and I
glided alone above the whole Mediterranean and saw
the yellow sun glinting on the domes and spires of
Venice.

There was one other consolation. Our daily rum
ration was used, illegally, to pay debts: "sippers" for
a routine favour, "gulpers" for something bigger,
and a whole tot if you'd saved someone's life. My
mate gave me gulpers from his cup and that, on top
of my own tot, made me find a corner behind a
locker on the upper deck where I "crashed my head"
until an unsympathetic petty officer flushed me out.

Sometimes, far out at sea, the ship would heave
to, a boat would be lowered to stand away from the
ship's side and the bosun's mate would pipe "Hands
over the side to bathe." Then we would strip off and
dive over. To lie in that bottomless, transparent
water which was indistinguishable from the sky was
as near to flying as I have ever been.

I'd heaved my marching boots overboard by this
time so that I couldn't be paraded among the
smartest, and the U-front of my tunic was down to

my navel. My cap ribbon had a sliding bow so that as I lined up for the liberty-boat to go ashore the bow was in the correct "pusser" position above the ear, but once ashore it slid around to be over one eye and therefore tiddley. And the tapes that tied the silk below the U were six inches on board but unfurled to dangle below the crutch once you'd stepped ashore. You weren't a matelot else.

Chopping and changing ships, I was never with any crew for long, but on *Chevron* I teamed up with an ex-tugboatman from Gravesend, not much older than me but already married, or at least engaged. Blakey had a double motto: "Nobody has boots big enough to scare me" and "The bigger they are the harder they fall" – and he stuck to it, both parts, many a time. With him I went out of bounds in Cyprus and Beirut, and where "the drinking of ouzo was strictly forbidden" we drank it.

I had bought a stuffed crocodile in Alex, a small one, and I kept it lashed up in my hammock with my *Complete Shakespeare* and *Modern Verse*, but at this time I was more interested in going ashore than in anything else. I saved Blakey from getting into trouble when I clung to his legs and stopped him leaping over a bar to get into a fight, but he wasn't there when I opened my mouth a bit too loud in Malta and I needed him most.

That night I learned the stupidity that underlies all tough films. Nobody gets up after even one good punch, and a broken tooth might be the least of your problems. That night I earned a cell with a wooden pillow, loss of leave and pay, and dental work that doesn't seem to have finished yet.

HOME AGAIN

England was unspeakably dreary. My homecoming began with the Bay of Biscay where the miracle of the blue sea and bright fishing boats went into reverse. The weather was bad and I was a passenger on an old minesweeper that kept breaking down and having to hoist two black spheres − the signal for "I am out of control" − as we wallowed in the grey-green troughs.

We docked in the rain and carried our kitbags and hammocks down the brow on to a black and greasy quayside. Everything was blurred by a cold drizzle, but one thing stood out − the battleship *King George V* lay at the quayside, a monster greyhound, sleek as a freak, and useless.

I had avoided a lot of the war, but in Greece I had seen a hillside still torn up by a battle, and a boy had shown us a slit trench where three British soldiers had "gone kaput"; I had wandered over the torn wreck of the *Duke of York* in Suda Bay "where the Stukas play" in the song I'd heard sailors sing; and alongside one crumbling jetty my destroyer had had to tie up to a shot-up German tank.

But battlefields and graves have a glamour that latecomers hope to share, and war becomes attractive in the telling. It takes lesser things, smaller symptoms, to show the deepness of the disease. I saw the signs from the train on my journey home.

Nothing had been painted for years – "there was a war on" so it hadn't mattered. Windows had not been cleaned, nor roads swept. There were queues everywhere waiting to hand over coupons for bread and meat and clothes. But none of that would have mattered if the drabness that had settled on everything had not also eaten into people.

I was a foreigner from a sunny clime and my home seemed to have crumbled into a place of ragged carpets and drooping curtains. My mother was worn and tired, dejection had caught hold of her, and my father was at the beginning of the long battle he had with tuberculosis. Only my sister Elizabeth and little Frank remained with them. They had so many troubles that my homecoming was subdued and I did not get the hero's welcome that I thought was my due. All that Mediterranean sunshine had culminated in a blocked drain.

Norman and David were in the Army, and Elizabeth would soon be a nurse. Frank, who was five, had had by far the worst of it and the war ended nothing for him. Throughout his childhood, while the rest of us were away, he would keep watch on Dad asleep in his chair terrified that at any moment he might die.

Back to barracks. Back to school. There was precious little difference. I was still making no decisions for myself. I was being fed, clothed and had a roof put over my head. For three and a half years I had been saying "Aye-aye, sir" to anything wearing gold braid, and back in barracks I had to buy new boots and polish them for a royal parade. A pair of princesses, as blue and pink as sugared almonds in a glass casket, wafted by as I presented arms to their Rolls Royce. I had been ordered to apply for the medal or medals we were all entitled to, but such medals are part of that alien pomp, so I never bothered.

My demob number came up. I collected my civvy suit and trilby hat, gave the hat to Frank to use as a cowboy stetson, took off my naval tunic by tearing it down the front, drank my gratuity and went looking for a job.

REPORTER

I wanted to write but nothing was coming. There were stories and poems and plays wherever I looked, but my pen would not put down the words. I had lost my nerve. The Navy was done with, my gratuity had given out, and I was arguing with my father again. I was back to where I had started.

There was the chance to apply for a place at university and get a grant as an ex-serviceman, but I turned it down. It was as though I was once more saying no to being a prefect, but this time I knew I was doing myself some damage. The truth was I'd lost all confidence and couldn't face more schooling. I was back to where I had been three years before, except that now I needed a job.

I had no idea what I wanted to do, but I applied for a place in a bank. It was an absolutely random decision because I certainly didn't want to work in one, but the bank itself saved me from the embarrassment of ever doing so. They didn't think a recently retired Acting Able Seaman was suitable.

A potato merchant had a vacancy for a warehouseman. It seemed ideal, lumping sacks of potatoes around while I sorted myself out, and I tried very hard to persuade him to take me, but he told me I had too much education.

There was no future for me in any respectable job, so I walked into the office of the *Wisbech Standard* and asked to be taken on. It was a long shot and I had very slight hopes so I did not allow myself to become very enthusiastic. But the editor, Wally Green, sat behind his desk with his hat on, and that did it. This was suddenly the real stuff of journalism, and I wanted it. He turned me down.

There were two papers in Wisbech. The *Standard* displayed itself in an office fronting the river; the *Isle of Ely and Wisbech Advertiser* lurked in a little street off the market place. I knew the *Advertiser* well because when I was still at school I had worked there on two nights a week helping to proofread advertisements. It had been dull work and I had no wish to try for it again, but I didn't have much choice.

However, things had changed at the *Advertiser*. The old guard had left, and David Newton had recently been appointed editor. He was small and dark and grey-suited, and he was a religious man whose children would conduct proper funeral services over dead birds. I knew that because he lived next door.

"Why didn't you come to me first, old man?" he asked.

I didn't like to say it was because I preferred Wally Green's office manners, so I mumbled something about not wanting to be a proofreader again.

In fact I had never actually corrected a proof; I had merely read out the text while somebody else made the corrections. Death notices had been my problem. The solemnity of them became so comical that by the time we came to the verses I would always collapse. I didn't have the kind of reverence David Newton expected, but he wasn't to know that.

"I hope you will be happy with us, old man," he said, and took me on as a reporter.

He was an extremely polite man, always washing his hands, but he threw me in at the deep end – which was what the annual meeting of a village football club was to me.

However, I wore a trench-coat, had a notebook in my pocket and a cigarette on my lip. I was a reporter ... except that I couldn't do shorthand, had never been to an annual meeting, and knew less than nothing about football. I sat through the minutes of the last meeting without taking a note, then the treasurer's report and the secretary's, and eventually "any other business" came up and still my notebook was a blank. I hadn't understood a word of what was going on.

But clubs meet in pubs – the only thing I ever enjoyed about football – and when it was all over I had a pint with the man from the *Standard*. He was the opposition, but he saved my life. I had been at school with Dennis Hammond and now he dictated his report to me, and I amended it a little and handed it in.

"Isn't it *thrilling* to see your stuff in print for the first time!" That was an elderly lady journalist when the first batch of papers reached the reporters' room.

"It certainly is," I said, and prayed that no one would compare it too closely with the *Standard*. It was Dennis who took the risk, however, for Wally

Green forbade his reporters to fraternize with the *Advertiser*. We did, but he didn't like it.

To get to the reporters' room at the *Advertiser* you had to go through the tunnel that separated the office from the gents outfitter next door, and climb a narrow stair from the back alley. The room must at one time have been part of somebody's home because it had a fireplace with a marble surround where a gas fire wheezed and popped, and most of the floor was taken up by a large dining-room table.

A great pile of newspapers, brittle and yellow with age, took up most of the table, and the heap was never ever moved except to clear a space for me at the edge. Printer's ink, old newsprint and gas gave the room an odour of decay that could never be dispersed because the one window opened only on to the crumbling brick of the narrow alleyway.

There were a couple of typewriters as heavy as upright pianos, but almost all copy was written in longhand on newsprint cut from old reel ends. There was a lot to do because the *Advertiser* came out twice a week and there was much space to fill. There was a recognized code to speed up penmanship – a single *o* stood for of, *t* for the, *tt* for that – but even then twenty or thirty pages for a single report were routine, as I was soon to find out.

The schoolboy sailor became a schoolboy reporter, but nobody trained me in anything. I had to pick it up by doing it except when it came to courts and councils, which were too tricky for someone who didn't know the ropes. I went along a few times as an observer before they let me loose.

Johnny Lawford, fresh out of the Army, was long

and lanky and loud and had a cavalier attitude towards council meetings that I envied. "There's not a lot in this, old sport," he'd say and then with dazzling speed he'd go through the minutes, rip out a couple of stories and start up a game of office cricket which was bound to bring in David Newton from the next room. "Could you keep the noise down a bit, old man?"

I was having to make many adjustments after the Navy, but I wasn't alone. Just about the entire editorial staff had been in the services. We had an army major who'd fought in the desert, a couple of sergeants and a Spitfire pilot. They had all been reporters before they joined up, and now they were getting back to being civilians, but every now and again there would be a mass departure to the Ship on the marketplace and anarchy would reign in the *Advertiser* office.

I was still, however, at the stage of having to ask for help even with wedding reports. We sent out forms for the brides to fill in the details, but often enough their spelling wasn't up to it so that I would read that someone was wearing a "tool" gown. This was some sort of fashion I didn't know about, so I had to ask our girl reporter, Meg Godfrey. She also had to tell me that the "freezer spray" one bride carried was flowers and not something to cool down the bridegroom.

The older lady journalist soon retired and Meg was the only girl we had. She was a feminist even then and had a strong line in indignation, which she needed in an office full of ex-servicemen.

Johnny would sometimes say that court cases

were boring – although he did enjoy the fat man accused of indecency who said in a little squeaky voice "It's them dirty pictures in the *News of the World* what done it!" But even traffic offences were a short story to me, and anything else was a novel.

A court is set up like a theatre, and I was never bored. It is often cruel. Whoever stands in the dock or the witness box – and a box it is, a lidless box in which the specimen is examined – always has layer after layer of pretence stripped away and in the end stands there naked. And magistrates can have their faults put on display just as easily. The chairman of the bench told one defendant who had just been found not guilty to "go away and not do it again".

Judges are frightening figures, and know it. A man who can send a message to an airfield to prevent the RAF sending aeroplanes over his court because the noise annoys him can easily make a timid witness, dazed by all the court procedure, quake with terror, and I often saw it done. It was the injustice of justice, and even now it is never reported because the menace is in the frown and the tone of voice and not in the words.

And the legal profession looks after its own. In a long dispute over a field boundary one of the barristers was so drunk he fell asleep, and when he got to his feet he was incoherent. The judge did not stop the case. He prompted the barrister, helping him along while the opposing counsel sorted out his papers for him. They would never have been as kind to a witness.

The barrister who drank was the same man who came into the office one day and I found him searching through the files. He was looking for the report of "a huge fire beside the river". I couldn't remember one, but he told me that his son, while playing with fireworks, had let off a "piece of atomic substance – and whoosh, the whole of the North Brink went up!"

I was hearing lots of stories, even if I wasn't writing them all.

PARSONS
PLEASURE

Every reporter had a list of regular calls he had to make. On Mondays I cycled round to see every clergyman in Wisbech and beyond, the Salvation Army major and the plump lady by the canal who was in touch with the Spiritualists.

Unexpectedly, parsons turned out to be a pleasure, especially those in the Church of England. One, a bachelor, was pursued by a large woman in his flock. He was the sort of man who really did wring his hands, and he did so as he bleated: "She was in my garden last night – tapping on the window!" But we both knew she was wasting her time; he was not exactly a ladies' man.

Another had come from Edith Sitwell's parish in Derbyshire. "Mad," he said. "I found her one day lying in a coffin with a lily in her hands. She told me she was trying to get atmosphere."

Chapel ministers were less easygoing; they had to be, because their congregations could always get rid of them if they became unpopular. However, the wife of one of them would often come to the door with a black eye, and I got into a fierce argument with another out in the Fens who tried to persuade me that black men were black because they bore the mark of Cain and that other shades of skin marked different levels of guilt. I saw him, years later, crouched in the corner of a café, mumbling over a bun, as small and dark and malevolent as one of the flies he told me he used to scorch to death in his slide projector as he attempted to get their image on the screen "for the kiddies in the Bible class".

But I heard Donald Soper, the Methodists' president, startle a congregation with the socialist implications of the Book of Amos, and a very jolly Baptist let me climb to the top of his steeple when it was being repaired. With one arm round the weather vane, I took aerial photographs of the town's rooftops and the flat fens beyond.

My shorthand was not good – nothing like that of Bob Easter, the Spitfire pilot, or George Usher, of the opposition, who could both take down every word of a council meeting in neat and tiny symbols while I would come away with pages of scrawl I couldn't read back. So I was more and more set to writing "specials", longish articles about people and places.

I wrote about a lady water diviner who was so accurate in her predictions that fruit-growers would hire her to help them decide where to dig wells in their orchards. She showed me where a stream ran under her kitchen and handed me her willow wand, but it refused to cut into my fingers and try to wrench itself free as it did when she held it.

There were bee-keepers who hired out hives to pollinate orchards, and one grower who declared war on the frosts that nipped the apple blossom. He not only had "smutch pots" that burned oily waste to lay a pall of warm smoke over his trees, but he also imported a tower from America that had high pressure burners which reflected heat over the treetops from a kind of umbrella. An outside thermometer was wired up to his bedside to tell him when to get up in the middle of the night to set the Fens alight.

I know how to make lattice-work icing because I interviewed an old man who had a reputation as a cake decorator. The front room of his cottage was very much like a village dressmaker's with finished creations waiting to be collected, half-clothed cakes on the sideboard, and scraps of lattice-work on patterns of greaseproof paper. His house had the cosy smell of a baker's shop.

I also watched another old man, a stonemason, cutting a finial cross for the roof of his village church. Shortly afterwards he was crushed to death by a bus, but the finial, a memorial without a name, still stands out against the sky.

We newshounds often hunted in pairs, a photographer and reporter together, and a friendly bellringer one day allowed us into his hanging chamber. This is the room at the top of the belfry where the bells are suspended. We went up the narrow spiral stairs in darkness and emerged into the dim, grey chamber where the only light filtered in through the slats of the louvres. We stood on a ledge overlooking the square pit in the floor where the bells, always left resting at the top of the swing, gaped up with black mouths like a nest of huge iron birds waiting to be fed.

The bellringer told us to wait, and disappeared downstairs. A moment later the largest of the black

mouths nodded in our direction, then swung down
and out of sight. Tons of dark metal moved without
a sound but then, just at the point where it began to
swing back towards us, the clapper fell against the
rim and the black mouth gave tongue. I have never
heard such a sound. That mass of ponderous metal,
ripped from the earth and forged and tortured into
shape, was a monster that came howling and clam-
mering for our blood. The sound went through us
and the tower rocked.

We ran for the daylight below and found the
ringer hauling on the rope and grinning like an ape.
It was only a mile or two away across the Fens to the
place where Dorothy L. Sayers had written *The Nine
Tailors,* in which a man is murdered by the sound
of bells. That captain of ringers knew very well what
bells could do.

Murders were few and far between, and almost
always a family affair. It was some time before I covered one, and I had moved beyond the edge of the
Fens by then. A woman, provoked beyond
endurance by a drunken husband who bullied her,
had shot him with his own shotgun when he came to
attack her one night. When the photographer and I
got there next morning there was drizzle that was
making the trees weep in the lane where it happened, but what I remember most of all was that the
couple had two small boys. They were being looked
after by a neighbour, but when we arrived they had
wandered into their own backyard and were near the
chicken run.

When I wrote up my report I did not say that I
had seen two boys, as pale as little white chickens

themselves, wandering near the place where their father lay dead and from which their mother had been taken away. They already had more problems than I had ever known, and I was not going to make it worse for them by describing them in a newspaper.

But if I had been writing a story, fiction, "making it up", I would certainly have set down what I had seen or, even more likely, I would have become one of those boys so that I also could live through their terrible night. Reporting has its uses, but fiction tells more of the truth, and I always knew where I would eventually go.

MOVING ON

In the reporters' room we made extra money by linage. Each of us was the recognized "correspondent" for one or more national newspapers and we would phone in any story we thought might make the grade and be paid so much a line if it appeared. It could be profitable. One of us, going to a garden party at Sandringham, saw the Queen Mother there but no other reporters. He shot off a roll of film with his own camera and sold it to *Picture Post* for fifty pounds, and they never used any of it.

Fifty quid could have bought a decent second-hand car, but normally we earned a lot less than a pound. I once made ten shillings for a report of a traffic offence which I sold to the man's local paper many counties away, but then felt that this was such a mean trick that I put it into a church box.

The bulk of linage came from football. Often I had to cover a football match for four evening papers – *Pink 'Uns* and *Green 'Uns* – at once. This meant phoning in so many words at stated intervals during the game, and it could be done only with the help of a runner. The press box at Fenland Park was no more than a wooden bench perched over the tunnel in the

stand, and the nearest phone was in a shack somewhere else.

I knew nothing about football, but I did get the
knack of stringing together phrases I'd picked up
and I could blather on about "a period of end-to-end
play ensued" or "the leather rattled the rigging"
during a "ding-dong battle" until the final whistle let
me off the hook.

Joe Barrett was sometimes my runner – which was
like asking Steve Davis to chalk my cue. Joe had
been my junior by a year or two at the Grammar
School where he'd been an athlete who broke
records, played every sport and was academically
brilliant into the bargain. He was also a natural
debunker. When I handed my copy down to him
from the press box he would read it back, loudly,
and pick out the choice bits: "What's this about
taking a penalty 'from close in', Gordon?"

Joe the debunker, fresh from the RAF, challenged
every journalistic assumption and was sometimes
laid back to the point of torpor, which didn't endear
him to some of the old hands but, except for sport,
he and I were in harmony, and still are.

I longed for book talk and found a kindred spirit
at an evening class in English Literature. It was run
by a Grammar School teacher, "Joe" Davy. I had not
known him at school but we'd go for a pint after the
class, he with his curly pipe and slouch hat, and talk
books and politics on the bridge after closing time.
He had a good rebellious nature and a passion for
words.

Treble Smith came back into my life. He was
clerking for a builder's merchant but studying the

piano with passion. I can't even remember whether
it was the Army or RAF he'd been in, so little had it
changed him, and we picked up on sixth form habits
three and a half years after they'd been interrupted.
It was a true case of arrested development.

We began a club, a literary and debating society
with dandyish pretensions. Members had to wear a
tie made of fur, and Treble was first in the field with
one cut from an old fur-lined glove of his mother's.
It hung in a bush beneath his thin face and pointed
nose, and made him look like a cross between a
squirrel and a ferret. He didn't care.

The society met in a pub on the North Brink,
and I delivered the first paper. It was on G. K.
Chesterton ... anybody who could write "a sense of
humour, a weird and delicate sense of humour, is the
new religion of the world" was the man for me. I
believed that our group should be something like the
society of revolutionaries in *The Man Who Was
Thursday* and be able to see that ordinary things are
miracles.

When I was still at school I'd sent away for the
Surrealist Manifesto and I'd kept to the spirit of it
with the crocodile and Shakespeare together in my
hammock. Now it was Treble and his fur tie. Our
society crumbled and Treble pursued respectability
and marriage with a kind of ferocious intensity,
although we would still go together to a canalside
pub where he would play the piano and switch suddenly from popular songs to Mozart.

There was a little knot of safe-robbers in the corner – I knew them through court cases – but they
quite liked Mozart. "He's a boy," they'd say. "Give

us another one, mate," and Treble got a pint on the piano.

There was a lot of safe-breaking in the Fens at that time because many fruit-growers had made huge profits during the war and their safes were stuffed with money that had never been declared for tax. Emptied safes were turning up in dykes and rivers, and one grower I knew about had a chest of drawers half full of notes which turned up when auctioneers were making an inventory.

We were overworked, but I was never bored, partly because I never read the paper; real boredom set in when I became a sub-editor and had to read it word for word. But I could cycle to three garden fêtes on a Saturday afternoon, take down the names of all the stallholders and find endless entertainment.

People provided it – such as the bowls club president who had a special voice for public occasions and at the end of one annual dinner said, "Hand we should 'ave 'earts of hice hif we didn't thank the hentertainers." But he laughed at himself; he was the town beadle and as he carried the mace in all his finery he would wink if he caught your eye. Next morning you would find him knocking down nails in the Corn Exchange floor, and he didn't consider it beneath his dignity.

I still was, always will be, a kind of teenager, but I had sooner or later, and it was already quite late, to seek something new.

One day David Newton called me into his office and said, "I'm a bit worried about some of our village correspondents, old man. The *Standard* is beating us to a lot of stories." He wanted me to cover one or two villages. "There's this chap Young at Upwell – we haven't had a thing from him for a long while."

I could have told him why. I knew Les Young never thought it worth his while to work for only a penny a line, but I was a bit embarrassed to say so.

"So if you could cycle out there once a week, old man, and call on a few people, I think things may improve."

"I'll do my best," I said, and I rang up the girl I was in love with. Sylvia was Les Young's daughter, and I married her.